The Revolutionary War in Lincoln and Gaston County

Compiled from:

SKETCHES OF WESTERN NORTH CAROLINA, HISTORICAL AND BIOGRAPHICAL

Illustrating Principally the Revolutionary Period of Mecklenburg,
Rowan, Lincoln and Adjoining Counties, Accompanied with Miscellaneous
Information, Much of It Never before Published

By

C. L. HUNTER

1877

Edited by: Stephen Payseur

The Revolutionary War in Lincoln and Gaston County

Compiled from:

SKETCHES OF WESTERN NORTH CAROLINA, HISTORICAL AND BIOGRAPHICAL

Illustrating Principally the Revolutionary Period of
Mecklenburg,
Rowan, Lincoln and Adjoining Counties, Accompanied with
Miscellaneous
Information, Much of It Never before Published

By

C. L. HUNTER

1877

Published by

CreekSide Publishing Company, PO Box 1848, Lincolnton NC
28093

ISBN-13:
978-1533484017

ISBN-10:
1533484015

Editor's Preface

I ran across the book, Sketches of Western North Carolina, by C.L. Hunter, several years ago when I was researching some other historical information. I found the book to be very interesting and containing facts that I had never heard or read before.

Since I was born and still live in Lincoln County, NC and much of my relations live there and in neighboring Gaston County, I was particularly drawn to those couple of chapters in Mr. Hunter's book.

I reasoned that there may be others who would like to know this information and stories concerning the part that our counties played in the Revolutionary War. We have all heard stories and read books and article about the War, but most of us have not gotten the details that Mr. Hunter presents. That reasoning resulted in this book.

What follows is C. L. Hunter's account of the Revolutionary War in both Lincoln and Gaston County. I haven't changed any of his words, I simply excerpted the chapters concerning these two counties. The only changes I have made, was in making the paragraphs shorter to make it easier to read. I have also added and Appendix to further clarify some of the items he wrote about.

I hope you find Hunter's account as interesting as I do.

Editor: Stephen Payseur, 2016

SKETCHES OF WESTERN NORTH CAROLINA, HISTORICAL AND BIOGRAPHICAL

Illustrating Principally the Revolutionary Period of Mecklenburg,
Rowan, Lincoln and Adjoining Counties, Accompanied with Miscellaneous
Information, Much of It Never before Published

By

C. L. HUNTER

1877

DEDICATION.

TO THE DESCENDANTS OF THE REVOLUTIONARY
PATRIOTS OF NORTH CAROLINA, WHETHER NOW
ABIDING WITHIN HER BORDERS AND SHARING
HER PROSPERITIES AND ADVERSITIES, OR
SCATTERED ABROAD IN OTHER STATES OF THE
AMERICAN UNION, BUT WHO STILL CHERISH A
LASTING VENERATION FOR THE MEMORIES OF
THEIR HEROIC FOREFATHERS; AND TO THE
YOUNG MEN OF THE STATE GENERALLY, WHO
WOULD DRAW LESSONS OF WISDOM, PATRIOTISM
AND ENDURANCE FROM THE EXAMPLES HEREIN
DESCRIBED, THIS VOLUME IS RESPECTFULLY
DEDICATED BY THE AUTHOR.

PREFACE.

History has been defined, "Philosophy teaching by example." There is no branch of literature in a republic like ours that can be cultivated with more advantage to the general reader than history. From the infinite variety of aspects in which it presents the dealings of Providence in the affairs of nations, and from the immense number of characters and incidents which it brings into view, it becomes a source of continuous interest and enjoyment.

The American Revolution is undoubtedly the most interesting event in the pages of modern history. Changes equally great and convulsions equally violent have often taken place in the Old World; and the records of former times inform us of many instances of oppression, which, urged beyond endurance, called forth the spirit of successful resistance. But in the study of the event before us—the story of the Revolution—we behold feeble colonies, almost without an army—without a navy—without an established government—without a good supply of the munitions of war, firmly and unitedly asserting their rights, and, in their defence, stepping forth to meet in hostile array, the veteran troops of a proud and powerful nation. We behold too, these colonies, amidst want, poverty and misfortunes, animated with the spirit of liberty and fortified by the rectitude of their cause, sustaining for nearly eight years, the weight of a cruel conflict upon their own soil. At length we behold them victorious; their enemies sullenly retiring from their shores, and these feeble colonies enrolled on the page of history as a *free, sovereign and independent nation.*

The American struggle for freedom, and its final achievement, was an act in the great drama of the world's history of such vast magnitude, and fraught with such momentous consequences upon the destinies of civilization throughout the world that we can scarcely ever tire in contemplating the instrumentalities by which, under Divine guidance it was effected. It has taught mankind that oppression and misrule, under any government, tends to weaken and ultimately destroy the power of the oppressor; and that a people united in the cause of freedom and their inalienable rights, are invincible by those who would enslave them.

No State in our Union can present a greater display of exalted patriotism, enduring constancy and persistent bravery than North Carolina. And yet, how many of our own people do we find who know but little of the early history of the State, her stern opposition to tyranny under every form, and her illustrious Revolutionary career.

On the shores of North Carolina the first settlement of English colonists was made; within her borders the most formidable opposition to British authority, anterior to the Revolution, was organized; by her people the *first declaration* of independence was proclaimed, and some of the most brilliant achievements took place upon her own soil.

For several years, at intervals, the author has devoted a portion of his time and attention to the collection of historical facts relating principally to Western North Carolina, and bordering territory of South Carolina, to whom, as a sister State, and having a community of interests, North Carolina frequently afforded relief in her hour of greatest need.

Such materials, procured at this late day—upon the arrival of our National Centennial year, are often imperfect and fragmentary in character—merely scattered facts and incidents gathered here and there from the traditional recollections of our oldest inhabitants, or from the musty records of our State and county offices; and yet, it is believed such facts, when truthfully transmitted to us, are worthy of preservation and rescue from the gulf of oblivion, which unfortunately conceals from our view much valuable information.

Being the son of a Revolutionary patriot, and accustomed in his boyhood to listen with enraptured delight to the narration of thrilling battle-scenes, daring adventures, narrow escapes and feats of personal prowess during the Revolution, all tending to make indelible impressions upon the tablet of memory, the author feels a willingness to "contribute his mite" to the store of accumulated materials relating to North Carolina, now waiting to be moulded into finished, historic shape by some one of her gifted sons.

Several of the sketches herein presented are original, and have never before been published. Others, somewhat condensed, have been taken from Wheeler's "Historical Sketches," when falling within the scope of this work. To the venerable author of that compilation, the author also acknowledges his indebtedness for valuable information furnished from time to time from the "Pension Bureau" at Washington City, relating to the military services of several of our Revolutionary patriots.

The author and compiler of these sketches only aspires to the position of a historian in a limited sense. It cannot be denied that the history of our good old State, modest in her pretensions, but filled with grand, patriotic associations, has never been fully written. Acting under this belief, he feels tempted to say, like Ruth following the reapers in the time of Boaz, he has "gleaned in the field until even," and having found a few "handfuls" of *neglected* grain, and beaten them out, here presents his "ephah of barley"—plain, substantial food it is true, but yet may be made useful *mentally* to the present generation, as it was *physically* of old, to the inhabitants of Palestine.

In conclusion, the author cherishes the hope that other sons, and daughters too, of North Carolina—some of them forming with himself, *connecting links of the past with the present*— will also become *gleaners* in the same field of research, abounding yet with scattered grains of neglected and unwritten history worthy of preservation.

If the author's efforts in this direction shall impart additional information, and assist in elucidating "liberty's story" in the Old North State, his highest aspirations will be gratified, and his agreeable labors amply rewarded.

LINCOLN COUNTY.

Lincoln County was formed in 1768, from Mecklenburg County, and named Tryon, in honor of William Tryon, at that time the Royal Governor, but his oppressive administration, terminating with cold-blooded murders at the battle of Alamance in 1771, caused the General Assembly in 1779 to blot out his odious name and divide the territory into Lincoln and Rutherford counties. These names were imposed during the Revolution when both of the honored heroes were fighting the battles of their country.

Lincoln County, separated from Mecklenburg by the noble Catawba river, has a Revolutionary record of peculiar interest. In June, 1780, the battle of Ramsour's Mill was fought, which greatly enlivened the Whigs, and, in a corresponding degree, weakened the Tory influence throughout the surrounding country.

In January, 1781, Lord Cornwallis, with a large invading army, passed through the county and camped for three days on the Ramsour battle-ground. General O'Hara, one of his chief officers, camped at the "Reep place," about two miles and a half west of Ramsour's Mill. Tarleton, with his cavalry, crossed the South Fork, in "Cobb's bottom," and passed over the ridge on which Lincolnton now stands (before the place had a "local habitation and a name,") in approaching his lordship's headquarters.

Although Lincoln county contained many who were misled through the artful influence of designing men, and fought on the *wrong side*, yet, within her borders were found a gallant band of unflinching patriots, both of German and Scotch-Irish descent, who acted nobly throughout the struggle for independence, and "made their mark" victoriously at Ramsour's Mill, King's Mountain, the Cowpens, and at other places in North and South Carolina.

Lincoln County, as Tryon, sent to the first popular Convention, which met at Newbern, on the 25th of August, 1774, Robert Alexander and David Jenkins. To Hillsboro, August 21st, 1775, John Walker, Robert Alexander, Joseph Hardin, William Graham, Frederick Hambright and William Alston. To Halifax, April 4th, 1776, James Johnston and Charles McLean. To the same place, November 12th, 1776, (which body formed the first State Constitution,) Joseph Hardin, William Graham, Robert Abernathy, William Alston and John Barber. Several of these names will be noticed in the subsequent sketches.

BATTLE OF RAMSOUR'S MILL.

The unsuccessful attempt made by General Lincoln to take Savannah, and the subsequent capture of the army under his command at Charleston, induced Sir Henry Clinton to regard the States of South Carolina and Georgia as subdued and restored to the British Crown. The South was then left, for a time, without any regular force to defend her territory. Soon after the surrender of Charleston, detachments of the British army occupied the principal military posts of Georgia and

14

South Carolina. Col. Brown re-occupied Augusta; Col. Balfour took possession of Ninety-Six, on the Wateree, and Lord Cornwallis pressed forward to Camden.

Sir Henry Clinton then embarked with the main army for New York, leaving four thousand troops for the further subjugation of the South. After his departure the chief command devolved on Lord Cornwallis, who immediately repaired to Charleston to establish commercial regulations and organize the civil administration of the State, leaving Lord Rawdon in command at Camden. North Carolina had not yet been invaded, and the hopes of the patriots in the South now seemed mainly to rest on this earliest pioneer State in the cause of liberty.

Charleston surrendered on the 12th of May, 1780. On the 29th of the same month Tarleton defeated Col. Buford in the Waxhaw settlement, upwards of thirty miles south of Charlotte, on his way to the relief of Charleston.

Just before the surrender, a well organized force from Mecklenburg, Rowan and Lincoln counties, left Charlotte with the same object in view, but arrived too late, as Charleston was then completely invested by the British army. And yet this force, after its return, proved of great service in protecting the intervening country, and prevented the invasion of North Carolina until a few weeks after the battle of Camden.

At this critical period General Rutherford ordered out the whole militia, and by the 3d of June about nine hundred men assembled near Charlotte. On the next day the militia were addressed by the Rev. Alexander McWhorter, the patriotic President of "Liberty Hall Academy," (formerly "Queen's Museum"), after which General Rutherford dismissed them, with orders to hold themselves in readiness for another call.

15

Major, afterward General, Davie having recovered from his wounds received at Stono, near Charleston, again took the field, and part of his cavalry were ordered to reconnoiter between Charlotte and Camden. Having heard that Lord Rawdon had retired with his army to Hanging Rock, General Rutherford moved from his rendezvous to Rea's plantation, eighteen miles north-east of Charlotte, to Mallard Creek. On the 14th of June the troops under his command were properly organized. The cavalry, sixty-five in number under Major Davie, were equipped as dragoons, and formed into two companies under Captains Lemmonds and Martin. A battalion of three hundred light infantry were placed under the command of General William Davidson, a regular officer, who could not join his Regiment in Charleston after that place was invested.

About five hundred men remained under the immediate command of General Rutherford. On the evening of the 14th of June he received intelligence that the Tories, under Col. John Moore, had embodied themselves in strong force at Ramsour's Mill, near the present town of Lincolnton. He immediately issued orders to Colonel Francis Locke, of Rowan; Major David Wilson, of Mecklenburg; also to Captains Falls, Knox, Brandon, and other officers, to raise men to disperse the Tories, deeming it unwise to weaken his own force until the object of Lord Rawdon, still encamped at Waxhaws, should become better known.

On the 15th General Rutherford advanced to a position two miles south of Charlotte. On the 17th he was informed Lord Rawdon had retired towards Camden. On the 18th he broke up his camp south of Charlotte, and marched twelve miles to Tuckasege Ford, on the Catawba River. On the evening of that day he dispatched an express to Col. Locke, advising him of his movements, and ordering him to unite with him (Rutherford) at Col. Dickson's plantation, three miles northwest of Tuckasege Ford, on the evening of the 19th or on the morning of the 20th of June. The express miscarried, in some unaccountable way, and never reached Colonel Locke.

When General Rutherford crossed the river on the evening of the 19th, it was believed he would march in the night, and attack the Tories next morning; but still supposing his express had reached Colonel Locke, he waited for the arrival of that officer at his present encampment in Lincoln county, where he was joined by Col. Graham's regiment. At ten o'clock at night of the 19th, Col. James Johnston, a brave officer, and well acquainted with the intervening country, arrived at Gen. Rutherford's camp. He had been dispatched by Colonel Locke from Mountain Creek, sixteen miles from Ramsour's Mill, to inform Gen. Rutherford of his intention of attacking the Tories next morning at sunrise, and requested his co-operation.

Gen. Rutherford, still expecting his express would certainly reach Col. Locke soon after Col. Johnston left his encampment on Mountain Creek, made no movement until early next morning.

In pursuance of the orders given to Col. Locke and other officers from headquarters at Mallard Creek, on the 14th of June, they quickly collected as many men as they could, and on the 18th Major Wilson, with sixty-five men, crossed the Catawba at Toole's Ford and joined Major McDowell, from Burke, with twenty-five horsemen. They passed up the river at a right angle with the position of the Tories, for the purpose of meeting other Whig forces. At McEwen's Ford, being joined by Captain Falls with forty men, they continued their march up the east side of Mountain Creek, and on Monday, the 19th, they united with Col. Locke, Captain Brandon and other officers, with two hundred and seventy men.

The whole force now amounted to nearly four hundred men. They encamped on Mountain Creek at a place called the *glades*. The officers met in council and unanimously agreed it would be unsafe to remain long in their present position, and, notwithstanding the disparity of the opposing forces, it was determined that they should march during the night and attack the Tories in their camp at an early hour next morning. It was said that the Tories being ignorant of their inferior force, and being suddenly attacked would be easily routed. At this time, Col. Johnston, as previously stated, was dispatched from Mountain Creek to apprise General Rutherford of their determination.

Late in the evening they commenced their march from Mountain Creek, and passing down the south side of the mountain they halted at the west end of it in the night when they again consulted on the plan of attack. It was determined that the companies under Captains Falls, McDowell and Brandon should act on horseback and march in front. No other arrangement was made, and it was left to the officers to be governed by circumstances after they reached the enemy. They accordingly resumed their march and by day light arrived within a mile of the Tories, assembled in strong force, about two hundred and fifty yards east of Ramsour's Mill, and half a mile north of the present town of Lincolnton.

The Tories occupied an excellent position on the summit of the ridge, which has a gentle slope, and was then covered with a scattered growth of trees. The foot of the hill on the south and east was bounded by a glade and its western base by Ramsour's mill pond, The position was so well chosen that nothing but the most determined bravery enabled the Whigs, with a greatly inferior force, to drive the Tories from it, and claim the victory of one of the most severely contested battles of the Revolution.

The forces of Colonel Locke approached the battle ground from the east, a part of his command, at least, having taken "refreshments" at Dellinger's Tavern, which stood near the present residence of B.S. Johnson, Esq., of Lincolnton. The companies of Captains Falls, McDowell and Brandon were mounted, and the other troops under Col. Locke were arranged in the road, two deep, behind them. Under this organization they marched to the battle-field. The mounted companies led the attack. When they came within sight of the picket, stationed in the road a considerable distance from the encampment, they perceived that their approach had not been anticipated. The picket fired and fled to their camp. The cavalry pursued, and turning to the right out of the road, they rode up within thirty steps of the line and fired at the Tories.

This bold movement of the cavalry threw them into confusion, but seeing only a few men assailing them they quickly recovered from their panic and poured in such a destructive fire upon the horsemen as to compel them to retreat. Soon the infantry hurried up to their assistance, the cavalry rallied, and the fight became general on both sides. It was in this first attack of the cavalry that the brave Captain Gilbraith Falls was mortally wounded in the breast, rode about one hundred and fifty yards east of the battle ground, and fell dead from his horse.

The Tories, seeing the effect of their fire, came a short distance down the hill, and thus brought themselves in fair view of the Whig infantry. Here the action was renewed and the contest fiercely maintained for a considerable length of time. In about an hour the Tories began to fall back to their original position on the ridge, and a little beyond its summit, to shield a part of their bodies from the destructive and unceasing fire of the Whigs. From this strong and elevated position the Tories,

19

during the action, were enabled at one time to drive the Whigs nearly back to the glade.

At this moment Captain Hardin led a small force of Whigs into the field, and, under cover of the fence, kept up a galling fire on the right flank of the Tories. This movement gave their lines the proper extension, and the contest being well maintained in the center, the Tories began to retreat up the ridge. Before they reached its summit they found a part of their former position in possession of the Whigs. In this quarter the action became close, and the opposing parties in two instances mixed together, and having no bayonets they struck at each other with the butts of their guns. In this strange contest several of the Tories were made prisoners, and others, divesting themselves of their mark of distinction, (a twig of green pine-top stuck in their hats), intermixed with the Whigs, and all being in their common dress, escaped without being detected.

The Tories finding the left of their position in possession of the Whigs, and their center closely pressed, retreated down the ridge toward the pond, still exposed to the incessant fire of the Whig forces. The Whigs pursued their advantages until they got entire possession of the ridge, when they discovered, to their astonishment, that the Tories had collected in strong force on the other side of the creek, beyond the mill. They expected the fight would be renewed, and attempted to form a line, but only eighty-six men could be paraded. Some were scattered during the action, others were attending to their wounded friends, and, after repeated efforts, not more than one hundred and ten men could be collected.

In this situation of affairs, it was resolved by Colonel Locke and other officers, that Major David Wilson of Mecklenburg, and Captain William Alexander of Rowan, should hasten to General Rutherford, and urge him to press forward to their assistance. General Rutherford had marched early in the morning from Colonel Dickson's plantation, and about six or seven miles from Ramsour's, was met by Wilson and Alexander.

Major Davie's cavalry was started off at full gallop, and Colonel Davidson's battalion of infantry were ordered to hasten on with all possible speed. After progressing about two miles they were met by others from the battle, who informed them the Tories had retreated. The march was continued, and the troops arrived at the battleground two hours after the action had closed. The dead and most of the wounded were still lying where they fell.

In this action the Tories fought and maintained their ground for a considerable length of time with persistent bravery. Very near the present brick structure on the battle-ground, containing within its walls the mortal remains of six gallant Whig captains, the severest fighting took place. They here sealed with their life's blood their devotion to their country's struggle for independence.

In addition to those from their own neighborhoods, the Tories were reinforced two days before the battle by two hundred well-armed men from Lower Creek, in Burke County, under Captains Whiston and Murray. Colonel John Moore, son of Moses Moore, who resided six or seven miles west of Lincolnton, took an active part in arousing and increasing the Tory element throughout the county.

He had joined the enemy the preceding winter in South Carolina, and having recently returned, dressed in a tattered suit of British uniform and with a sword dangling at his side, announced himself as Lieutenant Colonel in the regiment of North Carolina loyalists, commanded by Colonel John

Hamilton, of Halifax. Soon thereafter, Nicholas Welch, of the same vicinity, who had been in the British service for eighteen months, and bore a Major's commission in the same regiment, also returned, in a splendid uniform, and with a purse of gold, which was ostensibly displayed to his admiring associates, accompanied with artful speeches in aid of the cause he had embraced. Under these leaders there was collected in a few weeks a force of thirteen hundred men, who encamped on the elevated position east of Ramsour's Mill, previously described.

The Tories, believing that they were completely beaten, formed a stratagem to secure their retreat. About the time that Wilson and Alexander were dispatched to General Rutherford, they sent a flag under the pretense of proposing a suspension of hostilities for the purpose of burying the dead, and taking care of the wounded. To prevent the flag officer from seeing their small number, Major James Rutherford and another officer were ordered to meet him a short distance from the line. The proposition being made, Major Rutherford demanded that the Tories should surrender in ten minutes, and then the arrangements as requested could be effected.

In the meantime Moore and Welch gave orders that such of their own men as were on foot, or had inferior horses, should move off singly as fast as they could; so that, when the flag returned, not more than fifty men remained. These very brave officers, *before the battle*, and who misled so many of their countrymen, were among the first to take their departure from the scene of conflict, and seek elsewhere, by rapid flight, *more healthy quarters*. Col. Moore, with thirty of his followers, succeeded in reaching the British army at Camden, where he was threatened with a trial by court-martial for disobedience of orders in attempting to embody the Loyalists before the time appointed by Lord Cornwallis.

As there was no perfect organization by either party, nor regular returns made after the action, the loss could not be accurately ascertained. Fifty-six men lay dead on the side of the ridge, and near the present brick enclosure, where the hottest part of the fight occurred. Many of the dead were found on the flanks and over the ridge toward the Mill. It is believed that about seventy were killed altogether, and that the loss on either side was nearly equal. About one hundred were wounded, and fifty Tories made prisoners. The men had no uniform, and it could not be told to which party many of the dead belonged.

Most of the Whigs wore a white piece of paper on their hats in front, which served as a mark at which the Tories frequently aimed, and consequently, several of the Whigs, after the battle, were found to be shot in the head. In this battle, neighbors, near relatives and personal friends were engaged in hostile array against each other. After the action commenced, scarcely any orders were given by the commanding officers.

They all fought like common soldiers, and animated each other by their example, as in the battle of King's Mountain, a little over three months after. In no battle of the Revolution, where a band of patriots, less than four hundred in number, engaged against an enemy, at least twelve hundred strong, was there an equal loss of officers, showing the leading part they performed, and the severity of the conflict. They were all

"Patriots, who perished for their country's right,
Or nobly triumphed on the field of fight."

Of the Whig officers, Captains Falls, Knox, Dobson, Smith, Bowman, Sloan, and Armstrong were killed. Captain William Falls, who commanded one of the cavalry companies, was shot in the breast in the first spirited charge, as previously stated,

23

and riding a short distance in the rear, fell dead from his horse. His body, after the battle was over, was wrapped in a blanket procured from Mrs. Reinhardt and conveyed to Iredell (then a part of Rowan) for burial. Captain Falls lived in Iredell county, not far from Sherrill's Ford, on the Catawba.

There is a reliable tradition which states that when Captain Falls was killed a Tory ran up to rob the body, and had taken his watch, when a young son of Falls, though only fourteen years old, ran up suddenly behind the Tory, drew his father's sword and killed him. Captain Falls was the maternal grandfather of the late Robert Falls Simonton, who had the sword in his possession at the time of his death, in February, 1876.

Captain Patrick Knox was mortally wounded in the thigh; an artery being severed, he very soon died from the resulting hemorrhage. Captain James Houston was severely wounded in the thigh, from the effects of which he never fully recovered. Captain Daniel McKissick was also severely wounded, but recovered, and represented Lincoln county in the Commons from 1783 to 1787. Captains Hugh Torrence, David Caldwell, John Reid, all of Rowan county, and Captain Smith, of Mecklenburg, came out of the conflict unhurt. William Wilson had a horse shot down under him, and was wounded in the second fire. Several of the inferior officers were killed. Thirteen men from the vicinity of Fourth Creek [Statesville] lay dead on the ground after the battle, and many of the wounded died a few days afterward. Joseph Wasson, from Snow Creek, received five balls, one of which it is said he carried *forty years to a day*, when it came out of itself. Being unable to stand up he lay on the ground, loaded his musket, and fired several times.

The brick monumental structure on the southern brow of the rising battle-ground, about fifty or sixty yards from the present public road, contains the mortal remains of six Whig Captains; also those of Wallace Alexander, and his wife, who was a daughter of Captain Dobson, one of the fallen heroes on this hotly-contested field of strife.

The loss of the Tories was greater in privates, but less in officers, than the Whigs. Captains Cumberland, Warlick and Murray were killed, and Captain Carpenter wounded. Captains Keener, Williams and others, including Lieutenant-Colonel John Moore and Major Welch, escaped with their lives, but not "to fight another day."

On the highest prominence of the battle-ground, in a thinly-wooded forest, is a single headstone pointing out the graves of three Tories, probably subordinate officers, with the initials of their names inscribed in parentheses, thus: "[I.S.] [N.W.] [P.W.] "—with three dots after each name, as here presented. A little below are two parallel lines extending across the face of the coarse soap stone, enclosing three hearts with crosses between, as much as to say, *here lie three loving hearts*.

Near a pine tree now standing on the battle-ground, reliable tradition says a long trench was dug, in which was buried nearly all of the killed belonging to both of the contending forces, laid side by side, as the high and the low are perfectly equal in the narrow confines of the grave.

INCIDENTS OF THE BATTLE.

Early on the morning of the 20th of June, 1780, when the Tories were forming their forces in martial array near the residence of Christian Reinhardt, situated on the south-western brow of the battle-ground, he conducted his wife, with two little children in his arms, and several small negroes, across the creek to a dense cane-brake extending along and up the western bank of the mill pond as a place of safety. He then returned to his residence, and in a very short time the battle commenced.

As the contest raged, and peal after peal of musketry reverberated over the surrounding hills and dales, his dwelling-house, smoke-house, and even his empty stables were successively filled with the dead, the dying and the wounded. When the battle was nearly over, and victory about to result in favor of the Whigs, many of the Tories swam the mill pond at its upper end, and thus made their escape. Two of these fleeing Tories, with green pine tops in their hats, [their badge of distinction], rushed through the cane-brake very near to Mrs. Reinhardt and her tender objects of care, exclaiming as they passed. "We are whipped! we are whipped!!" and were soon out of sight.

During the unusual commotion and terrific conflict of arms, even the deer were aroused from their quiet retreat. One of these denizens of the cane-brake, with sprangling horns, dashed up near to Mrs. Reinhardt, and after viewing for a moment, with astonishment, the new occupants of their rightful solitude, darted off with a celerity little surpassing that of the fleeing Tories.

As soon as the firing ceased, Mrs. Reinhardt came out of her covert with her little ones, and, on reaching the bridge, at the mill, found it had been torn up by the retreating Tories, but, being met there by her husband, she was enabled to cross over, reach her home, and witness the mournful scene which presented itself. The tender sympathy of woman's heart, ever ready to minister to the wants of suffering humanity, was then called into requisition, and kindly extended. In a short time her house was stripped of every disposable blanket and sheet to wrap around the dead, or be employed in some other useful way. Neighbors and relatives, a few hours before bitter enemies, were now seen freely mingling together and giving every kind attention to the sufferers, whether Whig or Tory, within their power.

ROUTE OF THE BRITISH ARMY THROUGH LINCOLN COUNTY.

After the battle of the Cowpens, on the 17th of January, 1781, Lord Cornwallis left his headquarters at Winnsboro, S.C., being reinforced by General Leslie, and marched rapidly to overtake General Morgan, encumbered with more than five hundred prisoners, and necessary baggage, on his way to a place of safety in Virginia. His Lordship was now smarting under two signal defeats (King's Mountain and the Cowpens) occurring a little more than three months apart. But the race is not always to the swift nor the battle to the strong. "Man proposes, but God disposes."

The original manuscript journal of Lord Cornwallis, now on file in the archives of the Historical Society of the State University at Chapel Hill, discloses, with great accuracy, the movements of the British army through Lincoln, Mecklenburg and Rowan counties.

On the 17th of January, 1781, the headquarters of General Leslie were at Sandy Run, Chester County, S.C. On the 18th, at Hillhouse's plantation, in York County, he returns his thanks to the troops under his command, and informs them that all orders in future will issue from Lord Cornwallis and the Adjutant General. At eight o'clock at night, Lord Cornwallis issues his orders to the army to march at eight o'clock on the ensuing morning in the following order: 1. Yagers; 2. Corps of Pioneers; 3. two three pounders; 4. Brigade Guards; 5. Regiment of Bose; 6. North Carolina Volunteers; 7. two six pounders; 8. Lieutenant Colonel Webster's Brigade; 9. Wagons of the General; 10. Field Officers' wagons; 11. Ammunition wagons; 12. Hospital wagons; 13. Regimental wagons; 14. Provision train; 15. Bat. horses; a captain, two subalterns, and one hundred men from Col. Webster's Brigade, to form a rear guard. On the 19th the army camped at Smith's house, near the Cherokee Iron Works, on Broad river.

On the 20th the army camped at Saunder's plantation, on Buffalo creek. On the 23rd the army crossed the North Carolina line, and camped at Tryon old Court House, in the western part of the present county of Gaston. On the 24th the army arrived at Ramsour's Mill, near the present town of Lincolnton. Here Cornwallis was compelled to remain three days to lay in a supply of provisions for his large army. To accomplish this, foraging parties were sent out in different directions to purchase all the grain, of every kind, that could be procured. Ramsour's Mill, surrounded with a guard of eight or ten men, was set to work, running *day and night*, converting the grain into meal or flour.

General O'Hara camped at the "Reep place," two miles and a half northwest of Ramsour's Mill. His forces crossed the South Fork, about a mile above the bridge, on the public road leading to Rutherfordton. Tarleton's cavalry crossed the same stream in "Cobb's bottom," passing over the present site of Lincolnton, to form a junction with Cornwallis. This small divergence from the direct line of travel, and subsequent concentration at some designated point, was frequently made by sections of the British army for the purpose of procuring supplies.

Lord Cornwallis, during his transitory stay, made his headquarters nearly on the summit of the rising ground, two hundred and fifty yards east of the Mill, on which had been fought the severe battle between the Whigs, under Colonel Francis Locke, and the Tories, under Lieutenant Colonel John

Moore (son of Moses Moore), in which the former were victorious.

Christian Reinhardt, one of the first German settlers of the county, then lived near the base of the rising battle ground, and carried on a tan-yard. He owned a valuable servant, named Fess, (contraction of Festus,) whose whole *soul* was exerted in making good *sole* leather, and upper too, for the surrounding country. This servant, greatly attached to his kind master, was forced off, very much against his will, by some of the British soldiery on their departure; but his whereabouts having been found out, Adam Reep, and one or two other noted Whigs, adroitly managed to recover him from the British camp, a few days afterward, and restored him to his rightful owner.

The Marquee of Lord Cornwallis was placed near a a pine tree, still standing on the battle ground, left there by the present owner of the property, (W.M. Reinhardt, Esq., grand son of Christian Reinhardt,) in clearing the land, as a memento of the past—where Royalty, for a brief season, held undisputed sway, and feasted on the fat of the land.

Reliable tradition says that some of the British soldiery, while encamped on the Ramsour battle ground, evinced a notable propensity for depredating upon the savory poultry of the good old house-wife, Mrs. Barbara Reinhardt—in other words, they showed a fondness for procuring *fowl meat* by *foul means*, in opposition to the principles of honesty and good morals. As soon as the depredations were discovered by Mrs. Reinhardt she immediately laid in her complaints at head-quarters. Whereupon his lordship, placing greater stress upon the sanctity of the eighth commandment than his loyal soldiers, promptly replied, "Madam, you shall be protected," and accordingly had a guard placed over her property until his departure.

31

Another incident relating to the advance of the British army is to the following effect. As Tarleton's cavalry passed through the southern part of Lincoln county (now Gaston) they rode up to the residence of Benjamin Ormand, on the head-waters of Long Creek, and tied one of the horses, which they had taken, to the top of a small white oak, growing in his yard. This little Revolutionary *sapling* is still living in the serenity of a robust old age, and now measures, two feet from the ground, *twenty-seven feet in circumference!* Its branches extend all around in different directions from forty to fifty feet, and the tree is supposed to contain at least ten cords of wood.

When Tarleton's cavalry were on the point of leaving, they took the blanket from the cradle in which James Ormand, the baby, was lying, and used it as a saddle-blanket, and the large family Bible of Benjamin Ormand was converted into a *saddle!!*

The Bible was afterward found near Beattie's Ford, on the Catawba River, in the line of the British march, and restored to its proper owner. Mr. Z.S. Ormand, a grandson of Benjamin Ormand, and a worthy citizen of Gaston County, now lives at the old homestead, where the Bible, considerably injured, can be seen at any time, as an abused relic of the past, and invested with a most singular history. Tarleton's cavalry also seized and carried off the bedding and blankets in the house, and some of the cooking utensils in the kitchen.

Mr. Ormand also informs the author that he frequently heard his grandmother, who then lived near Steele Creek Church, say that she was present at the great meeting at Charlotte, on the 20th of May, 1775, and that she exhibited, on that occasion, *a quilt of her own manufacture.* She said it was a large turn out of people from all parts of the county, and was considered a suitable time for the *fair sex* to exhibit productions of their own hands.

Having replenished his commissary department as much as possible while encamped on the Ramsour battleground, and having experienced too much delay in his late march in consequence of the encumbrance of his baggage, Cornwallis destroyed, before moving, all such as could be regarded as superfluous. The baggage at head-quarters was first thrown into the flames, thus converting the greater portion of his army into light troops, with a view of renewing more rapidly the pursuit of Morgan, or of forcing General Greene into an early action.

It is said "pewter plates" were freely distributed among some "loyal" friends in the immediate vicinity, or thrown into the mill-pond; and large numbers of very strong glass bottles, originally filled with English ale, or *something stronger*, were broken to pieces on the rocks, fragments of which may be seen scattered around at the present time.

Thus disencumbered, Cornwallis, early on the morning, of the 28th of January, broke up camp and marched to the Catawba River, but finding it much swollen, and rendered impassable in consequence of heavy rains at its sources, he fell back to Forney's plantation, five miles from the river. Jacob Forney was a thrifty, well-to-do farmer, and a well-known Whig. The plantation is now (1876) owned by Willis E. Hall, Esq. Here the British army lay encamped for three days, waiting for the subsidence of the waters, and consumed, during that time, Forney's entire stock of cattle, hogs, sheep and poultry, with all of which he was well supplied. (For further particulars, see sketch of "Jacob Forney, Sen.")

Having dried their powder, and laid in an additional supply of provisions and forage, the British army was now prepared to renew more actively the pursuit of Morgan.

On the evening before the marching of the main army, Colonel Webster moved forward with the artillery, and a small detachment as a rear guard, and took position at Beattie's Ford. This was a mere feint, intended to create the impression that the whole British army would cross there, as it was the most eligible pass, and thus elude the vigilance of the Whigs.

At half-past two o'clock, on the morning of the 1st of February, 1781, Cornwallis broke up his camp at Forney's plantation, and marched to a private crossing-place known as Cowan's Ford, six miles below Beattie's Ford. As he approached the river, a little before the dawn of a cloudy, misty morning, numerous camp fires on the eastern bank assured him his passage would be resisted; but General Davidson had neglected to place his entire force, about three hundred and fifty in number, near the ford, so as to present an imposing appearance. As it was, only the companies of Captain Joseph Graham, and of two or three other officers, probably not more than one third of the whole force on duty, actually participated in the skirmish which immediately took place; otherwise, the result might have been far more disastrous to the British army.

The river at Cowan's Ford, for most of the distance across, has a very rugged bottom, abounding with numerous rocks, of considerable size, barely visible at the low water of summer time. With judicious forethought, Cornwallis had hired the services of Frederick Hager, a Tory, on the western bank, and, under his guidance, the bold Britons plunged into the water, with the firm determination of encountering the small band of Americans on the eastern bank.

Stedman, the English commissary and historian, who accompanied Cornwallis in his Southern campaigns, thus speaks of the passage of the river at Cowan's Ford:

"The light infantry of the guards, led by Colonel Hall, first entered the water. They were followed by the grenadiers, and the grenadiers by the battalions, the men marching in platoons, to support one another against the rapidity of the stream. When the light infantry had nearly reached the middle of the river, they were challenged by one of the enemy's sentinels. The sentinel having challenged thrice, and receiving no answer, immediately gave the alarm by discharging his musket; and the enemy's pickets were turned out. No sooner did the guide (a Tory) who attended the light infantry to show them the ford, hear the report of the sentinel's musket than he turned around and left them. This, which at first, seemed to portend much mischief, in the end, proved a fortunate incident. Colonel Hall, being forsaken by his guide, and not knowing the true direction of the ford, led the column directly across the river to the nearest part of the opposite bank."

This direct course carried the British army to a new landing-place on the eastern, or Mecklenburg side, so that they did not encounter a full and concentrated fire from the Whigs. Upon hearing the firing, General Davidson, who was stationed about half a mile from the ford, (in the Lucas house, still standing,) with the greater portion of the militia, hastened to the scene of conflict, evincing his well-established bravery, but it was too late to change the issue of the contest, and array any more effectual resistence. At this moment, General Davidson arrived near the river, and in attempting to rally the Whig forces for renewed action, received a fatal shot in the breast, fell from his horse, and almost instantly expired. The few patriots on the bank of the river nobly performed their duty, but had soon to retreat before vastly superior numbers.

The British infantry waded the river, preceded by their Tory guide, staff in hand, to show them the proper ford, and the statement made by some historians that General Davidson was killed by this guide is not corroborated by Stedman, the English historian; but, on the contrary, he leaves us to infer that the American General met his death at the hands of one of their own troops. The same authority states their own loss to be Colonel Hall and three privates killed, and thirty-six wounded.

The horse of Lord Cornwallis was fatally shot and fell dead just as he ascended the bank. The horse of General O'Hara, after tumbling over the slippery rocks several times, producing a partial submersion of his rider, finally reached the bank in safety. The British reserved their fire until they reached the eastern shore, and then pouring in two or three volleys into the ranks of the opposing Whig forces, now considerably disconcerted, soon compelled them to retreat with small loss.

Colonel Hall was buried on the edge of the alluvial land a short distance below the crossing-place, with a head and foot stone of rock from the adjoining hill, which were long visible and could be pointed out by the nearest neighbors; but these were finally concealed from view by successive overflows of sand from the swollen river. The privates of both contending forces were buried on the rising ground, near the scene of conflict, and with such haste on the part of the British interring party as to leave one of their mattocks behind them at the graves of their fallen comrades, eager to overtake the vigilant Morgan.

GEN. JOSEPH GRAHAM.

(Condensed from Wheeler's "Historical Sketches.")

General Joseph Graham was born in Pennsylvania on the 13th of October, 1759. His mother being left a widow with five small children, and slender means of support, removed to North Carolina when he was about seven years of age, and settled in the neighborhood of Charlotte. He received the principal part of his education at "Queen's Museum" in Charlotte, (afterward called "Liberty Hall Academy,") and was distinguished for his talents, industry and manly deportment.

His thirst for knowledge led him at an early period to become well acquainted with all those interesting and exciting events which preceded our Revolutionary struggle. He was present in Charlotte on the 20th of May, 1775, when the first Declaration of Independence was formally and publicly made. The deep impression made upon his mind by the solemn and illustrious decisions of that day gave good evidence that he was then preparing for the noble stand which he took during the war.

He enlisted in the army of the United States in May, 1778, at the age of nineteen years. He served in the Fourth Regiment of North Carolina regular troops, under Col. Archibald Lytle, acting as an officer in Captain Gooden's company. The troops to which he was attached were ordered to rendezvous at Bladensburg, Md. Having marched as far as Caswell county they received intelligence of the battle of Monmouth, when he returned home on a furlough.

He again entered the service on the 5th of November, 1778, and marched under General Rutherford to Purysburg, on the Savannah River, soon after the defeat of Gen. Ashe at Brier Creek. He was with the troops under Gen. Lincoln, and fought

37

in the battle of Stono, against Gen. Prevost, on the 20th of June, 1779, which lasted one hour and twenty minutes. During nearly the whole of this campaign he acted as quartermaster. In July, 1779, he was taken with the fever, and after two months' severe illness was discharged near Dorchester, and returned home.

After the surrender of Charleston, and defeat of Col. Bufort at the Waxhaw, he again entered the service as adjutant of the Mecklenburg Regiment, and spent the summer in opposing the advance of Lord Rawdon into North Carolina, and assailing his troops, then within forty miles of Charlotte.

When it was understood that the British were marching to Charlotte he was ordered by General Davidson to repair to that place, and take command of such a force as he could readily collect, and join Col. Davie. *About midnight* of the 25th of September, 1780, Col. Davie reached Charlotte. On the next day the British army entered Charlotte, and received such a *stinging* reception as to cause Lord Cornwallis to designate the place as the "Hornets' Nest of America." After a well-directed fire upon the British from the Court House to the gum tree, Gen. Graham, with the troops assigned to his command, retreated, opposing Tarleton's cavalry and a regiment of infantry for four miles on the Salisbury road. On the plantation formerly owned by Joseph McConnaughey, he again formed his men, and attacked the advancing British infantry. After again retreating, he formed on the hill above where Sugar Creek Church now stands. There, owing to the imprudent but honest zeal of Major White, they were detained too long, for by the time they had reached the crossroads a party of British dragoons were in sight, and, after close pursuit for nearly two miles, overtook them.

It was at this time that Lieut. George Locke, a brother of Col. Francis Locke, of Rowan County, was killed at the margin of a small pond, now to be seen at the end of Alexander Kennedy's lane. Between that spot and where James A. Houston now lives, Gen. Graham was cut down and severely wounded. He received nine wounds, six with the saber and three from musket balls. His life was narrowly and mercifully preserved by a large stock buckle which broke the violence of the stroke.

He received four deep gashes of the saber over his head and one in his side; and three balls were afterward removed from his body. After being much exhausted by loss of blood, he reached the house of the late Mrs. Susannah Alexander, where he was kindly nursed and watched during the night, and his wounds dressed as well as circumstances would permit. On the next day he reached his mother's residence, where the late Major Bostwick resided, and from that place transferred to the hospital in Charlotte.

Thus, at the tender age of twenty-one years, we see this gallant young officer leading a band of as brave men as ever faced a foe, to guard the ground first consecrated by the Mecklenburg Declaration of Independence, leaving his blood as the best memorial of a righteous cause, and of true heroism in its defence.

As soon as he recovered from his wounds, he again entered the service of his country. Gen. Davidson, who had command of all the militia in the western counties of the State, applied to him to raise one or more companies, promising him such rank as the number of men raised would justify. Through his great energy, perseverance and influence he succeeded in raising a company of fifty-five men in two weeks. These were mounted riflemen, armed also with swords, and some with pistols.

They supplied themselves with their own horses and necessary equipments, and entered the field without commissary or quartermaster, and with every prospect of hard fighting, and little compensation. After Tarleton's signal defeat at the Cowpens, Cornwallis resolved to pursue Gen. Morgan, encumbered with upwards of five hundred prisoners. At that time Gen. Greene had assumed command of the southern army, and stationed himself with a portion of it at Hicks' Creek, near to Cheraw.

After Gen. Morgan's successful retreat, Gen. Greene left his main army with Gen. Huger, and rode one hundred and fifty miles to join Gen. Morgan's detachment near the Catawba river. The plan of opposing Lord Cornwallis in crossing the Catawba was arranged by Gen. Greene, and its execution assigned to Gen. Davidson. Lieutenant Col. Webster moved forward and crossed the Catawba in advance with a detachment of cavalry co create the impression that the whole British army would cross there, but the real intention of Cornwallis was to make the attempt at Cowan's Ford. Soon after the action commenced, Gen. Davidson was killed, greatly lamented by all who knew him as a brave and generous officer. The company commanded by Gen. Graham commenced the attack upon the British as they advanced through the river, and resolutely kept it up until they ascended the bank. The British then poured in a heavy fire upon Graham's men, two of whom were killed. Col. William Polk and Rev. T.H. McCaule were near Gen. Davidson when he fell. Col. Hall and three or four of the British were killed and upwards of thirty wounded. The British were detained here about three hours in burying their dead and then resumed their march in pursuit of Gen. Morgan.

The body of General Davidson was secured by David Wilson and Richard Barry, conveyed to the house of Samuel Wilson,

Sen., there dressed for burial, and interred that night in the graveyard of Hopewell Church.

The North Carolina militia were then placed under the command of General Pickens, of South Carolina, and continued to harass the British as they advanced toward Virginia. General Graham with his company, and some troops from Rowan county, surprised and captured a guard at Hart's Mill, one mile and a-half from Hillsboro, where the British army then lay, and the same day joined Colonel Lee's forces. On the next day, under General Pickens, he was in the action against Colonel Pyles, who commanded about three hundred and fifty Tories on their way to join Tarleton.

These Tories supposed the Whigs to be a company of British troops sent for their protection, and commenced crying, "God save the King." Tarleton was about a mile from this place, and retreated to Hillsboro. Shortly afterward General Graham was in an engagement under Colonel Lee, at Clapp's Mill, on the Alamance, and had two of his company killed, three wounded and two made prisoners. Again, a few days afterward, he was in the action at Whitsell's Mill, under Colonel Washington. As the term of service of his men had expired, and the country was annoyed with Tories, General Greene directed him to return with his company and keep them in a compact body until they crossed the Yadkin, which they did on the 14th of March, 1781.

After the battle of Guilford the British retired to Wilmington, and but little military service was performed in North Carolina during the summer of 1781. About the 1st of September Fannin surprised Hillsboro and took Governor Burke prisoner. General Rutherford, who had been taken prisoner at Gates' defeat, was set at liberty, and returned home about this time. He immediately gave orders to General Graham, in whose military prowess and influence he placed great confidence, to raise a troop of cavalry in Mecklenburg County. These troops of dragoons, and about two hundred mounted infantry, were raised and formed into a legion, over which Robert Smith was made Colonel and General Graham Major.

They immediately commenced their march toward Wilmington. South of Fayetteville, with ninety-six dragoons and forty mounted infantry, made a gallant and successful attack against a body of Tories commanded by the noted Tory Colonels, McNeil, Ray, Graham and McDougal. This action took place near McFalls' Mill, on the Raft swamp, in which the Tories were signally defeated, their leaders dispersed, and their cause greatly damaged. In this spirited engagement one hundred and thirty-six Whigs opposed and vanquished six hundred Tories, reflecting great credit upon the bravery and military sagacity of General Graham.

A short time afterward he commanded one troop of dragoons and two of mounted infantry, and defeated a band of Tories on Alfred Moore's plantation, opposite Wilmington. On the next day he led the troops in person, and attacked the British garrison near the same place. Shortly afterward he commanded three companies in defeating Colonel Gagny, near Waccamaw Lake. This campaign closed General Graham's services in the Revolutionary war, having commanded in fifteen engagements with a degree of courage, wisdom, calmness and success, surpassed, perhaps, by no officer of the same rank.

Hundreds who served under him have delighted in testifying to the upright, faithful, and undaunted manner in which he discharged the duties of his trying and responsible station. Never was he known to shrink from any toil, however painful, or quail before any danger, however threatening, or stand back from any privations or sacrifices which might serve his country. After the close of the war he was elected the first Sheriff of Mecklenburg county, and gave great satisfaction by the faithful performance of the duties of that office. From 1788 to 1794 he was elected to the Senate from the same county. About the year 1787 he was married to Isabella, the second daughter of Major John Davidson. By this marriage he had twelve children. Not long after his marriage he removed to Lincoln county and engaged in the manufacture of iron. For more than forty years before his death he conducted a large establishment of iron works with great energy and success.

In 1814 General Graham commanded a Regiment of North Carolina Volunteers against the Creek Indians, and arrived about the time the last stroke of punishment was inflicted upon this hostile tribe by General Jackson, at the battle of the Horse Shoe. For many years after the war he was Major General of the 5th Division of the North Carolina Militia. By a life of temperance and regular exercise, with the blessing of God, he enjoyed remarkable health and vigor of constitution.

On the 13th of October, 1836, he made the following minute in his day-book: "This day I am seventy-seven years of age, *Dei Gratia.*" He rode from Lincolnton on the 10th of November, soon thereafter was struck with apoplexy, and on the evening of the 12th closed his eyes upon the cares and trials of a long, useful and honorable life.

General Joseph Graham was the father of the late Ex-Governor William A. Graham, one of North Carolina's most worthy, honorable, and illustrious sons.

BREVARD FAMILY.

(Condensed from Wheeler's "Historical Sketches.")

The Brevard family acted a very conspicuous part during our Revolutionary war. The first one of the name of whom anything is known was a Huguenot who fled from France on the revocation of the edict of Nantes in 1685, and settled among the Scotch-Irish in the northern part of Ireland. He there formed the acquaintance of a family of McKnitts, and with them set sail for the American shores. One of this family was a young and blooming lassie, "very fair to look upon." Brevard and herself soon discovered in each other kindred spirits, and a mutual attachment sprung up between them. They joined their fortunes, determined to share the hardships and trials incident to a settlement in a new country, then filled with wild beasts and savages. They settled on Elk river, in Maryland. The issue of this marriage were five sons and one daughter; John, Robert, Zebulon, Benjamin, Adam, and Elizabeth. The three elder brothers, with their sister and her husband, came to North Carolina between 1740 and 1750. The three brothers were all Whigs during the Revolution. John Brevard, whose family is the immediate subject of this sketch, married a sister of Dr. Alexander McWhorter, a distinguished Presbyterian minister from New Jersey, who had for a time the control of Queen's Museum in Charlotte. Soon after his marriage, Brevard also emigrated to North Carolina, and settled about two miles from Center Church, in Iredell county. Dr. McWhorter was a very zealous Whig, and it is said the British were anxious to seize him on account of his independent addresses, both in and out of the pulpit. But they failed in their endeavors, and, after the invasion of Charlotte by Cornwallis in 1780, he returned to the North.

At the commencement of the Revolutionary war, John Brevard, then an old and infirm man, had eight sons and four daughters, Mary, Ephraim, John, Hugh, Adam, Alexander, Robert, Benjamin, Nancy, Joseph, Jane and Rebecca. He was a well known and influential Whig, and early instilled his patriotic principles into the minds of his children. When the British army under Cornwallis passed near his residence a squad of soldiers went to his house and burned every building on the premises to the ground. No one was at home at the time except his wife, then quite old and infirm, the daughters having been sent to a neighboring house across a swamp to preserve them from any indignities that might be offered to them by a base soldiery.

When the soldiers came up a self-authorized officer drew a paper from his pocket, and after looking at it for a moment said, "these houses must be burned." They were accordingly set on fire. Mrs. Brevard attempted to save some articles of furniture from the flames, but the soldiers would throw them back as fast as she could take them out. Everything in the house was consumed. The reason assigned by the soldiery for this incendiary act was she then had "eight sons in the rebel army."

Mary, the eldest daughter of John Brevard, married Gen. Davidson who was killed at Cowan's Ford on the Catawba river.

Nancy married John Davidson. They were both killed by the Indians at the head of the Catawba river. Jane married Ephraim, a brother of John Davidson. Though very young, he was sent by Gen. Davidson, on the night before the skirmish at Cowan's Ford, with an express to Col, Morgan, warning him of the approach of the British forces.

Rebecca married a Jones and moved to Tennessee.

Ephraim Brevard, the eldest son, married a daughter of Col. Thomas Polk. After a course of preparatory studies he went to Princeton College. Having graduated, he pursued a course of medical studies and settled as a physician in Charlotte. Being highly educated, and possessed of a superior mind, and agreeable manner, he exerted a commanding influence over the youthful patriots of that day. In the language of Dr. Foote, "he thought clearly; felt deeply; wrote well; resisted bravely, and died a martyr to that liberty none loved better, and few understood so well." (For further particulars respecting Dr. Brevard, see Sketches of the Signers of the Mecklenburg Declaration.)

John Brevard, Jr., served in the Continental Army with the commission of Lieutenant, displaying, on all occasions, unflinching bravery and a warm devotion to the cause of American freedom.

Hugh Brevard, with several brothers, was at the battle of Ramsour's Mill. Early in the war he was appointed a Colonel of the militia, and was present at the defeat of General Ashe at Brier Creek. He settled in Burke county, and was elected a member of the Legislature in 1780 and 1781, was held in high esteem by his fellow citizens, and died about the close of the war.

Adam Brevard first served one year in the Northern Army under General Washington. He then came South, and was present at the battle of Ramsour's Mill. He there had a button shot from his pantaloons, but escaped unharmed. He was a blacksmith by trade, and, after the war followed this occupation for a considerable length of time. Being fond of reading he studied law in his shop, when not much pressed with business, and found a greater delight in the law-telling *strokes* of a Blackstone than in the hard-ringing strokes of a blacksmith's hammer.

He finally abandoned his trade and engaged in the practice of the law, in which he was successful. He was a man of strong intellect, sound judgment, and keen observation. He wrote a piece called the "Mecklenburg Censor," abounding with sarcastic wit and well-timed humor, making him truly the "learned blacksmith" of Mecklenburg county.

Alexander Brevard first joined the army as a cadet. He then received the commission of Lieutenant, and soon afterward that of Captain in the Continental Army. He was engaged in the battles of White Plains, Trenton, Princeton, Brandywine, Monmouth, and Germanton, and remained in the Northern Army under General Washington until some time in the year 1779, when, his health failing, he was sent into the country. After a short absence he reported himself for service to Gen. Washington. This illustrious and humane commander, seeing his slender figure and delicate appearance, remarked that he was unfit for hard service, and enquired of him where his parents lived. The reply was, in North Carolina. Gen. Washington then advised him to return home. With this advice he complied, and his health, in the meantime, having improved in the genial climate of Western North Carolina, he immediately joined the Southern Army under General Gates. Being a Captain in the regular service, and removed from his command, he was appointed quartermaster, and acted as such at the battle of Camden.

After the defeat of Gen. Gates, the Southern Army was placed under the command of Gen. Greene. Alexander Brevard was with this gallant commander in all his battles; so that, with little interruption, he was in active service *from the beginning to the end of the war*. He thought his hardest fighting was at the Eutaw Springs. He was there in command of his company, and in the hottest part of the fight, losing eighteen of his brave men. At one time he and his company were in a very critical situation. A division of the British army came very unexpectedly upon their rear while they were closely engaged in front; but, just at that moment, Col. Washington, perceiving their imminent danger, made an impetuous charge with his cavalry upon this division of the enemy. A portion of his men broke through, and formed again with the intention of renewing the charge. This was prevented by the retreat of the British into a position where it was impossible for the cavalry to pursue them.

Colonel Washington was unhorsed and made a prisoner, but succeeded with his brave men in preventing the meditated attack in the rear. Brevard had not observed this division of the enemy, and the first thing he saw was the flying caps and tumbling horses of the cavalry as they made their dashing charge upon them. This was the last important battle in which Capt. Brevard was engaged, fought on the 8th of September, 1781, and near the close of the war. On all occasions he maintained an unflagging zeal and promptitude of action in achieving the independence of his country, and evincing a persistent bravery unsurpassed in the annals of the American Revolution.

After the war Captain Brevard married Rebecca, a daughter of Major John Davidson, one of the signers of the Mecklenburg Declaration. Major Davidson suggested to himself and General Joseph Graham, another son-in-law, the propriety of entering into the manufacture of iron. They readily approved of the suggestion and went over into Lincoln County. There they found General Peter Forney in possession of a valuable iron ore bank.

With him they formed a copartnership and erected Vesuvius Furnace on the public road from Beattie's Ford to Lincolnton—at present known as Smith's Furnace. After operating for a time altogether, Forney withdrew. Davidson and Brevard then left Graham in the management of Vesuvius Furnace, and built Mount Tirzah Forge, now known as Brevard's Forge. The sons-in-law shortly afterward bought out Davidson, and finally they dissolved. Brevard then built a furnace on Leeper's Creek, above Mount Tirzah Forge, and continued in the iron business until his death.

Captain Brevard, being of a retiring disposition, never sought political favor, but preferred to discharge his obligations to his country rather by obeying than by making her laws. His manners were frank and candid, and the more intimately he was known the better was he beloved. The dishonest met his searching eye with dread, but the industrious and the honest ever found in him a kind adviser and beneficent assistant. Long will he be remembered as a pure man, a faithful friend, and an upright citizen, conscientious in the discharge of all his obligations and in the performance of all his duties. He was for many years, a worthy elder in the Presbyterian Church, and died, as he had lived, a true Christian, and with humble resignation, on the 1st of November, 1829, in the seventy-fifth year of his age. His mortal remains repose in a private cemetery, selected by General Graham and himself as a family burying ground, and near which has lately been built the church of Macpelah. He left seven children—Ephraim, Franklin, Harriet, Robert, Joseph, Theodore and Mary. Franklin and Joseph represented, at different times, the county of Lincoln in the State Legislature.

Joseph Brevard, the youngest son of John Brevard, Sen., at the youthful age of seventeen, held the commission of Lieutenant in the Continental army. His brother Alexander said he was at that time quite small and delicate, and that he always pitied him when it was his turn to mount guard. General ———, who was in command at Philadelphia, discovering that he wrote a pretty hand, appointed him his private secretary. In this position he remained until he received the commission of Lieutenant in the Southern army, which he held until the close of the war. After the war he studied law, and settled in Camden, S.C., where he took a high stand both as a lawyer and a citizen. After filling several offices of public trust, he was elected one of the Judges, which position he occupied with distinguished honor.

After a few years he resigned his Judgeship, and was twice elected to Congress from his district. He made a Digest of the Statute Laws of South Carolina, and also left one or two volumes of cases reported by himself. These books, particularly the latter, are still referred to as good legal authority. He died in Camden, and has left a name cherished and honored by all those who remember his numerous virtues.

Such is a brief and imperfect sketch of that family whose name is prefixed. Many events, of thrilling interest, connected with their revolutionary services, have, no doubt, sunk into oblivion; but enough has been presented to stimulate the rising generation to imitate their heroic example and admire their unfaltering devotion to the cause of American freedom.

COLONEL JAMES JOHNSTON.

Col. James Johnston, one of the earliest patriots of "Tryon," afterward Lincoln County, was born about the year 1742. His father, Henry Johnston, was of Scottish descent. During the many civil and ecclesiastical troubles which greatly agitated England preceding the ascent of William, Prince of Orange, to the throne in 1688, and the ruinous consequences of the defeat of Charles Edward, the "Pretender," at the battle of Culloden, in April, 1746, a constant tide of emigration was flowing from Scotland to the northern part of Ireland, or directly to the shores of the New World, then holding forth to the disturbed population of Europe peculiar features of attractiveness, accompanied with the most alluring prospects of future aggrandizement and wealth.

Among the families who passed over during this period were some of the extensive clan of Johnstons (frequently spelled *Johnstone*); also, the Alexanders, Ewarts, Bells, Knoxes, Barnetts, Pattons, Wilsons, Spratts, Martins, with a strong sprinkling of the Davidsons, Caldwells, Grahams, Hunters, Polks, and many others whose descendants performed a magnanimous part in achieving our independence, and stand high on the "roll of fame" and exalted worth.

The name Johnston in Scotland embraces many distinguished personages in every department of literature. From one of the families who came directly to America in 1722 ("Lord William Johnston") have descended in different branches, the late General Albert Sidney Johnston and General Joseph E. Johnston—illustrious, patriotic names the Southern people and a disinterested posterity will ever delight to honor.

The Johnstons in their native "land o'cakes and brither Scots," had the reputation of being "heady," strong-minded, proud of their ancestral descent, and were regarded, at times, as being rather "rebellious"—a trait of character which, in this last respect, some of their descendants strongly manifested in the late Confederate struggle, but in accordance with the most honorable and patriotic motives.

When Henry Johnston and his youthful wife settled on the western banks of the Catawba river, the country was then covered with its native forests, and over its wide expanse of territory, as yet but little disturbed by the implements of husbandry, the Indians and wild beasts held almost undisputed sway. The uplands were clothed with wild "pea vines," and other luxuriant herbage, and cattle literally roamed over and fed upon a "thousand hills." Every water course, too, bristled with cane-brakes, indicating the great fertility of the soil, and the sure road, under proper industrial efforts, to agricultural prosperity.

In the absence of family records we are left to infer Col. Johnston grew up to manhood, receiving as good an education as his own limited means and the opportunities of societies then afforded. It was then a gloomy period in our history. In 1765 the Stamp Act had been passed, which agitated the American Colonies from one extremity to the other. The dark cloud of discontent hung heavily over our people, too truly foreboding the storm of open rupture, and approaching revolution. During this exciting period he imbibed those patriotic principles, which, in subsequent years, governed his actions, and prepared him to cast in his lot, and heartily unite with those who pledged "their lives, their fortunes, and their sacred honor" in the cause of American freedom. He emphatically belonged to that class of ardent young men of the Revolutionary period

"Whose deeds were cast in manly mold,
For hardy sports or contest bold."

Tradition speaks of the wife of Henry Johnston as dying comparatively young, leaving two children—James, the immediate subject of this sketch, and Mary—who married Moses Scott, settled near Goshen Church, in the present county of Gaston, and there ended her days. Moses Scott had three children—James J., William and Abram Scott. Of these sons, James Johnston Scott married in 1803, Mary, a daughter of Captain Robert Alexander, a soldier of the Revolution, and of extensive usefulness. He (James) died in 1809, in the twenty seventh year of his age, leaving two children—Abram and Mary Scott, the former of whom in this Centennial year (1876) still survives, having nearly completed his "three-score years and ten."

Col. Johnston first entered the service as Captain of a company, in the winter of 1776, Col. William Graham commanding, against a large body of Tories in the northwestern section of South Carolina. This expedition is known in history as the "Snow Campaign," from the unusually heavy snow, of that winter, and, in conjunction with the troops of that State, drove the Tory commanders, Cunningham and Fletcher, from the siege of the post of Ninety Six. On the retreat of these Tory leaders they surprised and defeated them with a loss of four hundred of their followers. The reader may be curious to know the origin of the name "Ninety Six" applied to this post, now constituting the village of Cambridge, in Abbeville County. It was so called because it was ninety-six miles from the frontier fort, Prince George, on Keowee river, in the present county of Pickens. No portion of South Carolina suffered more during the Revolution than the district around Ninety-Six. The Tories were numerous, bold and vindictive, and for that reason the gallant Whigs of that region frequently

55

called upon their compatriots-in-arms in North Carolina, more particularly in Mecklenburg, Lincoln and Burke counties, for assistance in defending their homes and their property.

In this same year (1776) Gen. Rutherford called out a strong force of infantry and cavalry from Mecklenburg, Rowan, Tryon, (afterwards Lincoln), and other western counties to subdue the "Over-hill" Cherokee Indians, who were committing numerous depredations, and occasionally murdering the inhabitants on the frontier settlements. At that time the "Blue Ridge" constituted the bounds of organized civilization. The expedition, commanded by Gen. Rutherford, was completely successful, the Indians were routed, their towns destroyed, and a considerable number killed and made prisoners. Nothing short of this severe chastisement of the Indians for their depredations and murders would serve to teach them of the supremacy of the white man, and cause them to sue for peace. On this occasion many of the western patriots experienced their first essay in arms, and learned something of the toils and dangers of the soldier's life.

During the war several expeditions were sent from the border counties of North Carolina to assist in pulling down the Tory ascendancy of the disaffected portion of upper South Carolina. In one of these expeditions Col. Johnston experienced an adventure—a passage at arms, which, as an incident of the war and characteristic of his bravery, is here worthy of narration. On Pacolet river, near the place where the late Dr. Bivings erected a factory, Col. Johnston, in a skirmish, had a personal rencontre with Patrick Moore, a Tory officer, whom he finally overpowered and captured. In the contest he received several sword cuts on his head, and on the thumb of the right hand.

As he was bearing his prisoner to the Whig lines, a short distance off, he was rapidly approached by several British troopers. He then immediately attempted to discharge his loaded musket against his assailants, but unfortunately it *missed fire*, in consequence of blood flowing from his wounded thumb and wetting the *priming*. This misfortune on his part enabled his prisoner to escape; and, perceiving his own dangerous and armless position, he promptly availed himself of a friendly thicket at his side, eluded his pursuers and soon afterwards joined his command.

On the 14th of June, 1780, Gen. Rutherford, whilst encamped near Charlotte, received intelligence that the Tories under Col. John Moore had assembled in strong force at Ramsour's Mill, near the present town of Lincolnton. He immediately issued orders to Col. Francis Locke, of Rowan; to Major David Wilson, of Mecklenburg, and other officers, to use every exertion to raise a sufficient number of men to attack the Tories at that place.

On the 17th of June Gen. Rutherford marched from his encampment, two miles south of Charlotte, to the Tuckasege Ford, on the Catawba. He had previously dispatched an express to Col. Locke, advising him of his movement, and ordered him to join his army on the 19th or morning of the 20th of June, a few miles beyond that ford. The express, in some unaccountable way, miscarried. The morning of the 19th being wet, Gen. Rutherford did not cross the river until evening and encamped three miles beyond on Col. Dickson's plantation. Whilst there, waiting for Col. Locke's arrival, in obedience to the express, he received a notice from that officer, then encamped at Mountain Creek, informing him of his intention of attacking the Tories on the next morning at sunrise, and requested his co-operation. This notice was delivered to Gen. Rutherford by Col. Johnston at 11 o'clock of the night of the 19th of June, being selected for that duty by Col. Locke on account of his personal knowledge of the intervening country and undaunted courage. Col. Locke's encampment was then sixteen miles from Ramsour's Mill. Late in the evening of the same day, and soon after the departure of Col. Johnston to Gen. Rutherford's camp, Col. Locke marched with his forces, less than four hundred in number, stopped a short time in the night for rest and consultation, and arrived within a mile of Ramsour's at daylight without being observed by the Tories.

The battle soon commenced by the mounted companies of Captains Falls, McDowell and Brandon. The Tories at first fought with considerable bravery, driving back the Whig cavalry. These, however, soon rallied, and, being supported by the advancing infantry, pressed forward under their gallant leaders with a courage which knew no faltering and completely routed the Tories, driving them, after an hour's contest, from their strong position, and capturing about fifty of their number. This victory, occurring soon after the surrender of Charleston, when the Tories had become bold and menacing in their conduct, greatly cheered the Whigs throughout the entire South, animated them with fresh hopes, and nerved them on to future deeds of "noble daring."

Gen. Rutherford, not leaving his encampment at Col. Dickson's before daylight of the morning of the 20th of June, failed to reach Ramsour's Mill until two hours after the battle. Col. Johnston there joined his command, and participated in the closing duties of this victorious engagement in the cause of American freedom.

At the battle of King's Mountain Col. Johnston commanded the reserves, about ninety in number, which were soon called into service after the battle commenced. The decisive and brilliant victory of that memorable day has been so frequently adverted to in history that it is deemed here unnecessary to enter into particulars. Suffice it to say, it completely broke down the Tory influence in Western North Carolina, and its more rampant manifestations in upper South Carolina. It is known that Cornwallis, then in Charlotte, in a few days after hearing of the defeat and death of Ferguson, one of his bravest officers, marched from that rebellious town in the night and hastily retreated to safer quarters in Winnsboro, S.C.

During the progress of the war Col. Johnston was frequently engaged in other minor expeditions, requiring promptitude of action and unflinching bravery, in assisting to disperse bodies of Tories wherever they might assemble, and arrest obnoxious individuals when the peace and welfare of society demanded such service.

At the Provincial Congress which met at Halifax on the 4th of April, 1776, Colonel James Johnston and Colonel Charles McLean were the delegates from Tryon County. Colonel McLean was an early and devoted friend of liberty. He resided on the headwaters of Crowder's creek, in the present county of Gaston, and commanded the first regiment which marched from Lincoln county against the Tories of upper South Carolina. This Provincial Congress was one of the most important ever held in the State. The spirit of liberty was then in the ascendant, animating every patriotic bosom from the sea coast to the mountains. At this assembly the military organization of the State was completed, and the following patriotic resolution unanimously adopted:

> "*Resolved*, That the Delegates from this Colony
> in the Continental Congress be empowered to
> concur with the Delegates from the other
> colonies in declaring independence and forming
> foreign alliances, reserving to this colony the
> sole and exclusive right of forming a constitution
> and laws for this colony."

This early action of the Provincial Congress of North Carolina is the first public declaration, by proper legislative State authority, on record, preceding the Virginia resolutions of the same character by more than a month, and of those of the National Congress at Philadelphia by nearly three months, now exulting in its *centennial celebration*. Near the close of the Revolution Col. Johnston acted for a considerable length of time as disbursing agent for the Western Division of the army.

After the division of Tryon County in 1779 into Lincoln and Rutherford counties, he was elected to the Senate from the former county in 1780, '81 and '82. He also acted, for many years, as one of the magistrates of the county, and, by virtue of his office, was frequently called upon "*to make of twain one flesh* in the holy bonds of matrimony."

Major John Davidson, who knew Col. Johnston long and well, always summed up his estimate of his character by saying, "he was a most excellent man, and never shrunk from the performance of any duty when the welfare of his country demanded such service."

Several years previous to the Revolution Colonel Johnston married Jane Ewart, eldest daughter of Robert Ewart, a most worthy lady of Scotch-Irish descent. In 1775 Robert Ewart was appointed with Griffith Rutherford, John Brevard, Hezekiah Alexander, Benjamin Patton, and others, one of the Committee of Safety for the "Salisbury District," which included Rowan, Mecklenburg and other western counties. The marriage connections of other members of the Ewart family were as follows: Margaret married Joseph Jack; Mary married Robert Knox; Rachel married Thomas Bell; Betsy married Jonathan Price; Sallie married Thomas Hill; Robert married Margaret Adams.

At the battle of King's Mountain Robert Ewart, James Ewart, Robert Knox, Joseph Jack, Thomas Bell, Jonathan Price, Abram Forney, Peter Forney, and other brave spirits, were in the company commanded by Colonel James Johnston, and performed a conspicuous part in achieving the glorious victory on that occasion.

Previous to the war Colonel Johnston purchased valuable land on the Catawba river, one mile southwest of Toole's Ford, which became known in subsequent years as "Oak Grove" farm, deriving this name from several, native denizens of the forest which stood near the family mansion and cast around their beneficent shade. Here he was blest with a numerous offspring, and permitted to enjoy much of that dignified ease and pleasures of a quiet home-life which his patriotic services had assisted to procure. For many years preceding his death he was a consistent member and Ruling Elder of the Presbyterian Church at Unity, in Lincoln county. His large experience, general intelligence, disinterested benevolence, unsullied integrity and great decision of character, all combined to make him eminently useful in the different relations of society and secure for him the high regard and esteem of all who knew him.

Colonel Johnston died with calm resignation on the 23rd of July, 1805, aged about sixty-three years. His wife died on the 17th of August, 1795; and both, with other members of the family, are buried in a private cemetery on the "Oak Grove" farm.

GENEALOGY OF COL. JAMES JOHNSTON.

Col. James Johnston (sketch of his life and services previously given) married Jane Ewart, an estimable lady, daughter of Robert Ewart, of Scotch-Irish descent, and one of the early patriots of Mecklenburg County. Their descendants were, first generation:

1. Robert Johnston, who married Mary M, daughter of Capt. John Reid, a soldier of the Revolution, a Senator from Lincoln county in 1810 and 1811, and again in 1817 and 1818, and former proprietor of the Catawba Springs. He raised a family of twelve children, all of whom attained the age of maturity and survived their parents. The first death in the family was that of the late Rufus M. Johnston, of Charlotte. He was an industrious farmer, and upright member of society; for many years an elder of the Presbyterian church at Unity, and died with peaceful resignation on the 23rd of May, 1854, in the seventy-seventh year of his age. His wife, Mary died on the 30th of July, 1857, and both are buried in a private cemetery on the old homestead property, now owned by their grandson, John R. Johnston, Esq. His descendants were, 2d generation:

1. Sarah Johnston married Dr. Benjamin Johnson, of Virginia.

2. James A. Johnston married Jane Byers, of Iredell County.

3. Dr. Sidney X. Johnston married Harriet K. Connor, of Lincoln County.

4. Jane Johnston married first, John D. Graham, second, Dr. William B. McLean, of Lincoln County.

5. John R. Johnston married first, Delia Torrence, second, Laura E. Happoldt, of Burke County.

6. Robert Johnston married Caroline Shuford, of Lincoln County.

7. Dr. Thos. Johnston married Dorcas Luckey, of Mecklenburg County.

8. Harriet Johnston married William T. Shipp, of Gaston County.

9. Mary Johnston married Dr. William Davidson, of Mecklenburg County.

10. Martha Johnston married Col. J.B. Rankin, of McDowell County.

11. Col. William Johnston, present Mayor (1876) of Charlotte, married Ann Graham, of Mecklenburg County.

12. Rufus M. Johnston married Cecilia Latta, of York County, S.C.

2d. Margaret Ewart Johnston married Logan Henderson, Esq., youngest son of James Henderson, who moved from Pennsylvania to North Carolina at the first settlement of the country. He was the brother of Major Lawson Henderson, long and well known as one of the worthy citizens of Lincoln County, and of Col. James Henderson, a brave officer killed at the battle of New Orleans. The patriarchal ancestor, James Henderson, became the owner of a large body of land on the south fork of the Catawba River, in the present county of Gaston, embracing a valuable water-power, at which he erected a grist mill, then a new and useful institution. He lived to an extreme old age, and is buried on a high eminence near the eastern bank of the river, where a substantial stone wall surrounds the graves of himself, Adam Springs, the next owner of the property, and a few others.

In 1818, Logan Henderson joined the tide of emigration to Tennessee, and purchased much valuable land near Murfreesboro, in Rutherford County. In and near his last place of settlement, where most of his worthy descendants still reside. He died, after a brief illness, with calm composure, on the 8th of December, 1846, in the sixty-second year of his age. His wife survived him many years, and died with peaceful resignation on the 13th of August, 1863, in the seventy-fifth year of her age.

Their descendants were, second generation:

1. James F. Henderson married Amanda M. Vorhees, of Tennessee.

2. Violet C. Henderson married William F. Lytle, of Tennessee.

3. Jane E. Henderson married William S. Moore, of Tennessee.

The remaining children of Col. James Johnston were:

4. James Johnston, Jr., a promising young man, died near the age of maturity, in 1816, without issue.

5. Henry Johnston died in 1818 without issue.

6. Martha Johnston married Dr. James M. Burton. Soon after marriage they moved to Georgia, where they both died without issue.

7. Jane Johnston married Rev. John Williamson, pastor of Hopewell church, in Mecklenburg county, and died in 1817 without issue.

8. Catharine Johnston married John Hayes, Esq., who settled near Toole's Ford, on the Catawba River, about one mile from the old homestead of Col. James Johnston. He was a worthy Christian citizen, long a subject of patient suffering from disease, for many years an elder of the Presbyterian church, and died peacefully on the 13th of April, 1846, aged seventy-two years. His wife, Catharine, a lady of great amiability and worth, died on the 17th of December, 1858, aged seventy-four years.

Their descendants were, second generation:

1. Jane C. Hayes married Dr. Sidney J. Harris, of Cabarrus County.

2. Martha E. Hayes married William Fulenwider, of Lincoln County.

3. Margaret J. Hayes married Dr. William Adams, of York County, S.C.

4. Minerva W. Hayes married Col. William Grier, of Mecklenburg County.

5. Elizabeth L. Hayes married Charles L. Torrence, of Rowan County.

6. John L. Hayes married Matilda Hutchinson, of Mecklenburg County.

7. Dr. William J. Hayes married Isabella Alexander, great-grand daughter of John McKnitt Alexander, a Signer and one of the Secretaries of the Mecklenburg Convention of the 20th of May, 1775.

8. Dr. William Johnston, youngest son of Col. James Johnston, married Nancy, daughter of Gen. Peter Forney, of Lincoln County.

Their descendants were, second generation:

1. Annie C. Johnston married Dr. Joseph W. Calloway, of Rutherford County.

2. Jane C. Johnston died at school in Greensboro, Guilford County.

3. Martha S. Johnston married Richard R. Hunley, Esq., of Alabama.

4. Capt. James F. Johnston, citizen of Charlotte.

5. Susan L. Johnston, citizen of Charlotte.

6. William P. Johnston, (died young).

7. Margaret Johnston married Col. Peter F. Hunley, of Alabama.

8. Gen. Robert D. Johnson married Johncie Evans, of Greensboro, N.C.

9. Dr. William H. Johnston married Cathleen Gage, of Chester county, S.C.

10. Capt. Joseph F. Johnston married Theresa Hooper, of Alabama.

11. Catharine Johnson died comparatively young.

12. Bartlett S. Johnston, now (1876) a merchant of New York City.

Most of the descendants of Colonel James Johnston performed a soldier's duty, and won military distinction in the late war between the States, but our prescribed limits forbid a more extended notice of their Confederate services. This will be the noble task of some future historian, illustrating, as it would, much heroic bravery, chivalric daring, and perseverance under difficulties seldom surpassed in the annals of any people.

The preceding sketch and genealogy will serve to perpetuate the name and indicate the relationship of different branches of the family. It should awaken in every descendant emotions of veneration for the memory of a common patriarchal ancestor, who was one of the earliest and most unwavering patriots of the Revolutionary struggle for independence; contributed largely in council and in the field to its success, and whose mortal remains, with others of the family, now repose in the private cemetery of the "Oak Grove" farm, in Gaston county, N.C.

JACOB FORNEY, SR.

(Condensed from Wheeler's "Historical Sketches.")

Among the early settlers of Lincoln county (formerly Tryon) was Jacob Forney, Sr. He was the son of a Huguenot, and born about the year 1721. His life was checkered with a vicissitude of fortunes bordering on romance. At the revocation of the edict of Nantes, in 1685, his father fled from France, preferring self-expatriation to the renunciation of his religious belief, and settled in Alsace, on the Rhine where, under the enlightening influences of the reformation, freedom of opinion in matters of conscience was tolerated.

The family name was originally spelt *Farney*, but afterwards, in Alsace, where the German language is generally spoken, was changed to *Forney*. Here his father died, leaving him an orphan when four years old. At the age of fourteen he left Alsace and went to Amsterdam in Holland. Becoming delighted whilst there with the glowing accounts which crossed the Atlantic respecting the New World, and allured with the prospect of improving his condition and enjoying still greater political and religious privileges, he came to America by the first vessel having that destination, and settled in Pennsylvania.

Here he remained industriously employed until his maturity, when he returned to Germany to procure a small legacy. Having adjusted his affairs there he again embarked for America on board of a vessel bringing over many emigrants from the Canton of Berne in Switzerland. Among the number was a blithesome, rosy-cheeked damsel, buoyant with the chains of youth, who particularly attracted young Forney's attention. His acquaintance was soon made, and, as might be expected, a mutual attachment was silently but surely formed between two youthful hearts so congenial in feeling, and similarly filled with the spirit of adventure. Prosperous gales quickly wafted the vessel in safety to the shores of America, and soon after their arrival in Pennsylvania Jacob Forney and Mariah Bergner (for that was the fair one's name) were united in marriage. At this time the fertile lands and healthful climate of the South were attracting a numerous emigration from the middle colonies. Influenced by such inviting considerations, Forney joined the great tide of emigration a few years after his marriage, and settled in Lincoln County (formerly Tryon) about the year 1754.

The first settlers of Lincoln County suffered greatly by the depredations and occasional murders by the Cherokee Indians. On several occasions many of the inhabitants temporarily abandoned their homes, and removed to the more populous settlements east of the Catawba River. Others, finding it inconvenient to remove, constructed rude forts for their mutual defence. A repetition of these incursions having occurred a few years after Forney's arrival, he removed his family to a place of safety east of the river until the Indians could be severely chastised by military force.

On the next day he returned to his former residence, accompanied by two of his neighbors, to search for his cattle. After proceeding about a mile from home they spied a small Indian just ahead of them running rapidly, and not far from the spot now well known as the "Rocky Spring Camp Ground." Forney truly suspected more Indians were in the immediate vicinity. After progressing but a short distance, he and his party discovered, in an open space beyond them, ten or twelve Indians, a part of whom, at least, were armed with guns, apparently waiting their approach. Forney being a good marksman, and having a courage equal to any emergency, was in favor of giving them battle immediately, but his two companions overruled him, contending it would be impossible to disperse such a large number. It was therefore deemed advisable to retreat, and make their way to the fort, about two miles in their rear, where several families had assembled. After proceeding a short distance the Indians approached somewhat nearer and fired upon the party but without effect.

Forney directed his companies to reserve their fire until the Indians approached sufficiently near to take a sure and deadly aim, and maintain an orderly retreat in the direction of the fort. Soon after they commenced retreating the Indians again fired upon them and unfortunately one of the party, Richards, was dangerously wounded. At this critical moment, when one or two well directed fires might have repulsed their enemy, the courage of F——, the other companion, failed him, and he made his *rapid departure*.

Forney, however, continued his retreat, assisting his wounded companion as much as he could, and, although fired upon several times, managed to keep the Indians at some distance off by presenting, his unerring rifle when their timidity was manifested by falling down in the grass, or taking shelter behind the trees, each one, no doubt, supposing the well-aimed shot might fell him to the earth.

At length poor Richards, becoming faint from loss of blood, and seeing the imminent danger of his friend's life, directed Forney to leave him, and, if possible, save himself. This advice he reluctantly complied with and pursued his course to the fort. But the Indians did not pursue him much farther, being probably satisfied with the murder of the wounded Richards.

In this unequal contest Forney only received a small wound on the back of his left hand, but, on examination, discovered that

71

several bullets had pierced his clothes. This adventure shows what cool, determined bravery may effect under the most discouraging circumstances, and that, an individual may sometimes providentially escape although made the object of a score of bullets or other missiles of destruction. When he reached the fort he found the occupants greatly frightened, having heard the repeated firing.

After this adventure and narrow escape became generally known, a belief was widely entertained by the surrounding community that Forney was *bullet-proof*. It was even affirmed, and received *additions by repeating*, that after he reached the fort and unbuttoned his vest, a *handful of bullets dropped out*. In subsequent years Forney was accustomed to smile at this innocent credulity of his neighbors but frequently remarked that the impression of his being *bullet-proof* was of great service to him on more than one occasion preceding and during the Revolutionary war.

Few persons during the war suffered heavier losses than Jacob Forney. By persevering industry and strict economy he had surrounded himself and family with all the comforts, and, to some extent, luxuries of the substantial farmer. When Cornwallis marched through Lincoln County in the winter of 1781, endeavoring to overtake Morgan with his large number of prisoners captured at the Cowpens, he was arrested in his progress by the swollen waters of the Catawba river. Being thus foiled in his expectations, supposing he had Morgan *almost in his grasp*, Cornwallis fell back about five miles from the river to Forney's plantation, having been conducted there by a Tory well acquainted with the neighborhood. Here Cornwallis remained encamped for three days, consuming, in the meantime Forney's entire stock of cattle, hogs, sheep, geese, chickens, a large amount of forage, forty gallons of brandy, &c. His three horses were carried off, and many thousands of rails and other property destroyed.

But the extent of his losses did not end here. Cornwallis had been informed that Forney had a large amount of money concealed somewhere in his premises, and that if diligent search were made it might be readily found. This information set the British soldiers to work, and, aided by the Tory conductor's suggestions, they finally succeeded in finding his gold, silver and jewelry buried in his distillery, the greater portion of which he had brought with him from Germany. Whilst this work of search was going on without, his Lordship was quietly occupying the upper story of the family mansion, making it his headquarters. Forney and his wife being old, were *graciously* allowed the privilege of living in the basement.

As soon as he was informed his gold, silver and jewelry were found, amounting to one hundred and seventy pounds sterling, he was so exasperated for the moment that he seized his gun and rushed to the stair steps with the determination to kill Cornwallis, but his wife quickly followed and intercepted him, thus preventing the most deplorable consequences—the loss of his own life, and perhaps that of his family.

But the prudent advice of his wife, "Heaven's last, best gift to man," had its proper, soothing effect, and caused him to desist from his impetuous purpose. It is hardly necessary to inform the reader he was punished in this severe manner because he was a zealous supporter of the cause of freedom, and his three sons were then in the "rebel army."

The log house in which his lordship made his headquarters for *three days* and *four nights* is still in existence, though removed, many years since, from its original site to a more level location in the immediate vicinity. In this humble building he, no doubt, cogitated upon the speedy subjugation of the "rebels," and that subsequent glorification which awaits the successful hero. Little did Cornwallis then allow himself to think that he and his whole army, in less than nine months from that time, would have to surrender to the "rebel army," under Washington, as prisoners of war!

It is said Cornwallis, after finishing his morning repast upon the savory beef and fowls of the old patriot's property, would come down from his headquarters, up stairs and pass along his lines of soldiers, extending for more than a mile in a northwest direction, and reaching to the adjoining plantation of his son Peter, who kept "bachelor's hall," but was then absent, with his brother Abram, battling for their country's freedom.

About midway of the extended lines, and only a few steps from the road on which the British army was encamped, several granite rocks protrude from the ground. One is about four feet high, with a rounded, weather-worn top—a convenient place to receive his lordship's cloak. Another rock, nearly adjoining, is about two feet and a half high, with a flat surface gently descending, and five feet across. At this spot Cornwallis was accustomed to dine daily with some of his officers upon the rich variety of food seized during his stay, and washing it all down, as might be aptly inferred, with a portion of the forty gallons of captured brandy previously mentioned. This smooth-faced rock, on which his lordship and officers feasted for three days, is known in the neighborhood to this day as "Cornwallis' Table." On visiting this durable remembrance of the past quite recently, the writer looked around for a piece of some broken plate or other vessel, but sought in vain. The only mementoes of this natural table he could bear away were a few chips from its outer edge, without seriously mutilating its weather-beaten surface, now handsomely overspread with *moss* and *lichen*.

Where once the tramp and bustle of a large army resounded, all is now quiet and silent around, save the singing of birds and gentle murmurs of the passing breeze in the surrounding forest.

After Cornwallis left, Forney ascertained that the Tory informer was one of his near neighbors with whom he had always lived on terms of friendship. Considering the heavy losses he had sustained attributable to his agency, he could not overlook the enormity of the offence, and accordingly sent a message to the Tory that he must leave the neighborhood, if not, he would shoot him at *first sight*.

The Tory eluded him for several days by lying out, well knowing that the stern message he had received *meant action*. At length Forney, still keeping up his search, came upon him unawares and *fast asleep*. He was immediately aroused from his slumbers, when beholding his perilous situation, he commenced pleading most earnestly for his life, and promised to leave the neighborhood. Forney could not resist such touching appeals to his mercy, and kindly let him off. In a few days afterward the Tory, true to his promise, left the neighborhood and never returned.

Jacob Forney, Sr., died in 1806, aged eighty-five. In his offspring flowed the blood of the Huguenot and the Swiss— people illustrating in their history all that is grand in heroic suffering and chivalric daring. His wife survived him several years; both were consistent and worthy members of the Lutheran Church, and are buried in the "old Dutch Meeting House" graveyard, about three miles from the family homestead, and near Macpelah Church.

GEN. PETER FORNEY.

Gen. Peter Forney, second son of Jacob Forney, Sr., was born in Tyron County (now Lincoln) in April, 1756. His father was the son of a French Huguenot, and his mother Swiss. His origin is thus traced to a noble class of people whose heroic bravery, unparalleled suffering and ardent piety are closely connected in all lands where their lots have been cast with the promotion of civil and religious liberty.

Gen. Forney was one of the earliest and most unwavering Whigs of the revolutionary struggle. He first entered the service about the first of June, 1876, in Capt. James Johnston's company and Col. William Graham's regiment. The command marched to Fort McFadden, near the present town of Rutherfordton, and found that the greater portion of the inhabitants had fled for protection against the Cherokee Indians. After remaining a short time at the fort, he joined a detachment of about one hundred men in pursuit of the Indians, under Captains Johnston, Cook and Hardin.

They marched about one hundred miles, and not being able to overtake them, the detachment returned to the fort. In 1777, Gen. Forney volunteered as a Lieut. in Capt James Reid's company, for the purpose of quelling a considerable body of Tories assemble not far from the South Carolina line. The detachment was commanded by Col. Charles M'Lean, who marched into South Carolina and pursued after the Tories until it was ascertained Gen. Pickens, considerably in advance with his forces, had commenced the pursuit of the same, and was too far ahead to be overtaken. The detachment then returned to North Carolina, and, having taken several prisoners on the way, suspected of being inimical to the American cause, Capt. Reid was ordered to convey them to Salisbury. Gen. Forney still remained in service, and attached himself to Capt.

Kuykendal's company until some time in June. After this time he was frequently out in short expeditions for the purpose of intimidating and keeping down the rising spirit of the Tories, and arresting them, whenever the good of the country seemed to require it. In the fall of 1779 Gen, Forney volunteered with a party to go to Kentucky (Harrod Station) and after staying there a short time returned home.

At this time, there being a call made upon the militia to march to the relief of Charleston, he volunteered as a Lieut. in Capt. Neals' company, which was ordered to rendezvous at Charlotte, whilst there, waiting for the assemblage of more troops, he was appointed Captain by Col. Hampton and Lieut. Col. Hambright, Capt. Neal being superseded in his command on account of intemperance. From Charlotte the assembled forces march by way of Camden to Charleston, under the command of Cols. Hall, Dickson and Major John Nelson, continental officers. The militia of North Carolina, at the time, was commanded by Gen. Lillington. The term of service of Gen. Forney's company having expired shortly after his arrival at Charleston, and the British being in considerable force off that city, he induced the greater portion of his company to again volunteer for about six weeks longer, until fresh troops, then expected, would come to their relief.

In the spring of 1780 Gen. Forney, immediately after his return from Charleston, volunteered under Lieut. Col. Hambright, and went in pursuit of Col. Floyd a Tory leader on Fishing Creek, S. C. Hearing of their approach Floyd hastily fled to Rocky Mount, and the expedition, not being able to accomplish anything more at that time, returned to North Carolina. On the night of his arrival at home Gen. Forney was informed that the Tories, under Col. John Moore, were embodied in strong force at Ramsour's Mill near the present town of Lincolnton. On the next day he left home and went up the Catawba River, when, encountering a considerable body of Tories near Mountain Creek, he returned and immediately hastened to inform Gen. Rutherford. He found him encamped at Col. Dickson's, three miles northwest of Tuckaseege Ford, with a strong force. He then attached himself to his army, and marched early next morning to Ramsour's, but did not reach there until two hours after the battle, the Tories having been completely defeated by Col. Locke and his brave associates.

The dead and wounded were still lying where they had fallen, and Gen, Rutherford's forces assisted in the closing duties of that brilliant victory. Never afterwards in that county did Tory-loyalism present a formidable opposition to the final success of the American arms. Of the Whig officers the brave Captains Falls, Dobson, Smith, Knox, Bowman, Sloan and Armstrong were killed, and Captains Houston and McKissick wounded. Of the Tories, Captains Murray, Cumberland and Warlick were killed, and Capt. Carpenter wounded.

During the latter part of the year 1780 Gen. Forney was almost constantly in service in different portions of county. When Cornwallis entered the county in the last week of January, 1781, endeavoring to overtake Gen. Morgan with his prisoners captured at the Cowpens, he was providentially arrested in his march by the swollen waters of the Catawba river. He then fell back and encamped three days on the plantation of Jacob Forney, Sr., a well to-do farmer and *noted Whig*, consuming in the meantime, destroying or carrying off, every thing of value belonging to father or son, (Gen. Forney,) consisting of three horses, a large stock of cattle, hogs, sheep, fowls, forage, &c.

After the British army moved from this encampment, Gen. Forney commanded a company and placed themselves on the eastern bank of the river, endeavoring to oppose their crossing, and remained there until the light troops, under Col. Hall, effected a passage at Cowan's Ford. The militia being repulsed, and Gen. Davidson killed, he fled to Adam Torrence's, hotly pursued by Tarleton's troop of cavalry. At this place he found a considerable body of militia, but in great confusion in consequence of the death of Gen. Davidson, and greatly disheartened.

After giving the British one discharge of their arms, and killing several, the militia were repulsed, with small loss, and fled in all directions. Gen. Forney then retreated across the Yadkin, and remained on Abbot's creek about six weeks, during which time he had no regular command, and co-operated with other soldiers, whenever it appeared any advantage could be rendered to the American cause.

In the spring of 1871, Gen. Forney commenced repairing his plantation which the British had entirely destroyed, together with that of his father's in the immediate vicinity, whilst encamped there. He remained at home until a call was made upon the militia to march to the relief of Wilmington, when he again volunteered and commanded a company of dragoons, associated with Captains White and Lemmonds. In this expedition Charles Polk was appointed Major of dragoons, Gen. Rutherford in chief command, and marched through the disaffected country around Cross creek, (now Fayetteville,) and on to the immediate vicinity of Wilmington. Here Gen. Rutherford created a belief before his arrival that his forces were much larger than they really were. In consequence of this belief Major Craig, in command of the post, deeming his situation then insecure, immediately evacuated Wilmington and fled to Charleston. This was the only post in North Carolina held by the British, and with the flight of Craig all military operations ceased within her borders. This campaign closed the Revolutionary services of a gallant soldier and faithful patriot in the cause of American freedom.

In 1783 Gen. Forney married Nancy, daughter of David Abernathy, a lady of great moral worth and Christian benevolence. The natural goodness of her heart made her the "cheerful giver." Her numerous acts of charity were free of all ostentation, and flowed silently forth like gentle streams from a pure fountain, imparting new vigor and refreshing everything in their course.

After the close of the war, full of youthful enterprise, and anxious to engage in some useful business, he fortunately became the owner of the "Big Iron Ore Bank," seven miles east of Lincolnton. This is one of the best and most extensive deposits of iron ore, of the variety known as "magnetic," in the State.

Aware of the inexhaustible supply of ore, Gen. Forney disposed of interests to other parties (Brevard and Graham) and they immediately proceeded to erect a furnace (called Vesuvius) on Anderson's creek, now owned by the heirs of the late J.M. Smith, Esq. After a few years the copartnership was dissolved, separate sites were purchased by Forney and Brevard, on Leeper's creek, additional furnaces were erected and thus the manufacture of cast metal, under its various forms, was vigorously and successfully carried into operation. Gen. Forney commenced building his ironworks in 1787, associated for several years with his brother Abram, laid in a supply of the necessary stock, (ore and coal,) as recorded in a small account book, produced hammered iron in his forge on the 28th of August, 1788. This is believed to be the *first* manufacture of iron in the western part of the State. Here Gen. Forney permanently settled for life, and prospered in his useful calling. His residence received the name of "Mount Welcome," an appellation appropriately bestowed, as his future history manifestly proved. The poor and needy of his own neighborhood were frequently the beneficiaries of his bounty;

and the weary traveler was at all times made "welcome," and entertained beneath his hospitable roof "without money, and without price."

Gen. Forney was elected as a member to the House of Commons from 1794 to 1796 inclusively, and to the State Senate in 1801 and 1802. He was again called out from the shades of private life and elected as a Representative to Congress from 1813 to 1815. He also served as Elector in the Presidential campaigns of Jefferson, Madison, Monroe and Jackson. With these repeated evidences of popular favor his public services ended. Frequent solicitations were tendered to him afterwards, all of which he declined.

The infirmities of old age were now rapidly stealing upon him, and rendering him unfit for the proper discharge of public duties. For several years previous to his decease his mental vigor and corporeal strength greatly failed. After a short illness, without visible pain or suffering, he quietly breathed his last on February 1st, 1834, in the seventy-eighth year of his age. Generosity, candor, integrity and freedom from pride or vain show were prominent traits in his character. Let his name and his deeds and his sterling virtues be duly appreciated and faithfully imitated by the rising generation.

MAJOR ABRAM FORNEY.

Major Abram Forney, youngest son of Jacob Forney, Sr., was born in Tryon county, (now Lincoln) in October, 1758. His father was a Huguenot, and his mother Swiss. His origin is thus connected with a noble race of people who were driven into exile rather than renounce their religious belief under the persecutions which disgraced the reign of Louis XIV, of France. Major Forney first entered the service about the 25th of June, 1776, as one of the drafted militia in Capt. James Johnston's company, and Col. William Graham's regiment.

His company was then ordered to reinforce the troops at Fort McFadden, near the present town of Rutherfordton, and remained there until about the 1st of August, when he returned home to prepare for the expedition against the Cherokee Indians. The militia of Mecklenburg, Rowan, Lincoln and other counties were called out by orders from Gen. Rutherford, who marched to Pleasant Gardens, where he was joined by other forces. From that place Major Forney marched into the Nation with a detachment under Col. William Sharpe as far as the Hiwassee river, where they met with a portion of Gen. Williamson's army from South Carolina. The expedition was completely successful; the Indians were routed, their towns destroyed, a few prisoners taken, and they were compelled to sue for peace. The prisoners and property taken by Gen. Rutherford's forces were turned over to Gen. Williamson, as falling within his military jurisdiction. The expedition then left the Nation, and he reached home on the 13th of October, 1776.

In February, 1777, Major Forney again volunteered as a private in Capt. James Reid's company for the purpose of quelling some Tories who had, or were about to embody themselves near the South Carolina line. The detachment was commanded by Col. Charles McLean. The Tories were commanded by a certain John Moore, whom Col. McLean pursued into South Carolina until he ascertained Gen. Pickens was engaged in the same pursuit, and too far ahead to be overtaken. The detachment then returned to North Carolina, and having taken several prisoners on the way, suspected of being inimical to the American cause, Major Forney was ordered to take them to Salisbury. After this service he was dismissed and returned home in April, 1777.

At different times subsequently Major Forney volunteered in several short expeditions as far as the South Carolina line, for the purpose of intimidating and keeping down the rising spirit of the Tories, who were numerous in this section of country, and required a strict vigilance to hold them in a state of subjection. Early in June, 1780, when a call was made upon the militia, he volunteered in Capt. John Baldridge's company, marched to a temporary rendezvous at Ramsour's, and thence to Espey's, where they joined other troops under the command of Col. William Graham and Lieut. Col. Hambright. The united forces then proceeded to Lincoln "old Court House," near Moses Moore's, the father of Col. John Moore, the Tory leader, and marched and countermarched through that section of country.

At this time, hearing that Ferguson was coming on with a strong force, it was deemed advisable to retreat and cross the Catawba at Tuckaseege Ford. Col. Graham then marched with his forces to that place, and there met some other troops from South Carolina, under Col. Williams, retreating before Cornwallis, whose army had just reached Charlotte. The two forces then united under Col. Williams and marched up the west side of the Catawba river, and thence across the country in a circuitous direction towards South Carolina in the rear of Ferguson, and thus were enabled to fall in with the "over mountain" troops under Campbell, Shelby, Cleaveland, Sevier, and others, at the Cowpens, afterwards rendered famous by the battle fought there. The officers having agreed upon the plan of operations, a select portion of the combined forces marched rapidly in pursuit of Ferguson, and found him encamped on King's Mountain on the 7th of October, 1780. The action immediately commenced, and resulted in one of the most decisive victories gained during the Revolutionary struggle, and constitutes the *turning point* of final triumph in the cause of American freedom. Soon after the battle, Major Forney and Capt. James Johnston were appointed to number the dead on the British side.

They soon found Ferguson at the foot of the hill, dead, and covered with blood. His horse having been shot from under him, he continued to advance, sword in hand, cheering on his men by word and example, until five or six balls pierced his body and sealed his fate. Major Forney often stated he picked up Ferguson's sword, intending to keep it as a trophy, but some subordinate officer getting hold of it, made off with it, and thus deprived him of his prize. An incident connected with the closing scenes of this memorable battle is here worthy of being recorded:

As Major Forney was surveying the prisoners, through the guard surrounding them, he spied one of his neighbors, who only a short time before the battle had been acting with the Whigs, but had been persuaded by some of his Tory acquaintances to join the king's troops. Upon seeing him Major Forney exclaimed, "is that you, Simon?" The reply quickly came back, "Yes, it is, Abram, and I beg you to get me out of this *bull pen*; if you do, I will promise never to be caught in such a scrape again." Accordingly, when it was made to appear on the day of trial that he had been unfortunately wrought upon by some Tory neighbors, such a mitigation of his disloyalty was presented as to induce the officers holding the court-martial to overlook his offence and set him at liberty. Soon afterward, true to his promise, he joined his former Whig comrades, marched to the battle of Guilford and made a good soldier to the end of the war.

Near the close of the year 1780, hearing that Col. Morgan was preparing to go upon an expedition into South Carolina, Major Forney attached himself to the command of Capt. James Little, with the intention of joining his forces, but did not come up with them until after the battle of the Cowpens. He then returned home, and remained there until the 27th of January, 1781, when all the Whigs in his section of the country had to fly before Cornwallis in pursuit of Morgan with his large number of prisoners on their way to Virginia. Major Forney then crossed the Catawba, and joined a detachment of troops on its eastern bank under Capt. Henderson, placed as a guard by Gen. Davidson at Cowan's Ford, where it was expected the British might attempt to cross.

Having stood guard for some time at this point, and being relieved, he went a short distance to a house to procure refreshments of which he was much in need, and was not present when the guard was repulsed, and Gen. Davidson killed. He then fled with the other troops to Adam Torrence's, about ten miles distant, where a considerable body of militia had assembled, but were greatly disheartened on account of the death of Gen. Davidson. The day was damp and unfavorable to the use of firearms. The militia, without much order, fired once at the British, killing seven, and then dispersed in all directions. He then retreated until he reached Gen. Greene's army, in Guilford county. From this place he was advised to return home, and in doing so was furnished with a ticket to procure provisions on the way.

On the 25th of March, 1781, the militia being again called out, Major Forney attached himself to the command of Capt. Samuel Espey, acting as a Sergeant. The company then joined a detachment of militia under Gen. Thomas Polk, marched into South Carolina, and came up with Gen. Greene's army at Rugeley's Mill. The army was then placed under the command of Col. Dudley, and remained under him until Gen. Greene commenced his march to the post of Ninety Six. At this time, Capt. Espey being compelled to leave the service in consequence of a wound received at the battle of King's Mountain, went home with a part of his company, and then Major Forney joined the command of Capt. Jack, still acting as Sergeant. Soon afterward the expedition returned to Charlotte, when he was dismissed by Capt. Jack, about the 1st of July, 1781.

In a short time afterward, Major Forney attached himself to the company of Capt. John Weir, under orders to proceed to Wilmington. His company crossed the Catawba at Tuckaseege Ford on the 1st day of November, 1781, and encamped three or four miles beyond the river on the road leading to Charlotte.

On the next day the company marched through Charlotte and encamped at Col. Alexander's, who had been ordered to take command of the detachment. Whilst there intelligence was received of the return of Gen Rutherford's forces. Major Forney was then sent to that officer for orders; receiving these, the company recrossed the Catawba. Capt. Loftin then took command in place of Capt. Weir, who had resigned and returned home. The company proceeded to form several stations in the county, and arrested some *suspected* persons. Capt. Thomas McGee having assumed command in place of Loftin, resigning, marched with the prisoners to Salisbury, and delivered them up to the proper authorities on the 31st of December, 1781.

Again, when a call was made upon the militia in 1782, to march against the Cherokee Indians, Major Forney was placed in command of a company, and ordered to rendezvous at Ramsour's Mill. He remained there from about the 1st of June until the 1st of August, when he marched to the head of the Catawba and joined the troops of Burke and Wilkes. He then attached his company to Col. Joseph McDowell's regiment, marched across the Blue Ridge and met with the Rutherford troops on the Swannanoa river, under the command of Col. Miller. After the junction of the Rutherford troops, the expedition, under Gen. Charles McDowell, marched into the Nation, nearly on the trail of Gen. Rutherford in 1776, but proceeded some farther than where his army halted. The expedition was entirely successful; took a few prisoners, returned home and were dismissed in October, 1782.

This was the last service of a brave soldier, who fought long, and fought well, for the freedom of his country. Major Abram Forney died on the 22nd day of July, 1849, in the ninety-first year of his age.

His only surviving son, Capt. Abram Earhardt Forney, at the present time, (1876,) is still living at the old homestead, has already passed his "three score years and ten;" is an industrious farmer, and worthy citizen of Lincoln county.

REMARKS.

Among the curious revolutionary mementoes that Capt. A.E. Forney, son of Major Abram Forney, has in his possession is a small *leather memorandum pocket-book*, filled originally with twenty-four blank leaves; also a *powder horn*, made by his father preparatory to an expedition to the mountains. The front, or opening sides, is handsomely ornamented with numerous small stars, arranged diagonally across the surface and around the borders. The back side has the patriot's initials, A.F. distinctly impressed, and immediately beneath, the year 1775, the whole displaying considerable artistic skill; numerous entries appear on its pages, made at different times, and without reference to strict chronological order; brief notices of military and agricultural matters and occasionally a birth, death or marriage are harmoniously blended. On page 5 is this entry: "The first snow in the year 1775, was on December the 23rd day, and it was very deep."

On the same page it is recorded: "April the 28th day, Old John Seagle departed this world, 1780." On page 11 this entry appears: "May the 3rd day I sowed flax seed in the year 1779," and other entries relating to the same agricultural avocation are interspersed through the little book. The culture of flax was then an indispensible employment. Our soldiers then wore *hunting shirts*, made of flax, to the battle fields.

Cotton was not generally cultivated until twenty years later. On page 24 it is recorded: "May the 1st day there was a frost in the year 1779." On page 22 is this entry: "Be it remembered the battle between the Whigs and Tories (at Ramsour's) was fought on the 20th day of June 1780." (Signed) Abram Forney. Had any doubt arisen as to the precise date of this important battle it could have been ascertained from this memorandum pocket-book of this distinguished patriotic soldier. On page 13 is an entry which, on its realization, sent a thrill of joy throughout the land: "April the 17th day, great talk of peace in the year 1783." The definite treaty was not signed until the 30th of September following, and a new Republic sprung into existence.

GENEALOGY OF THE FORNEY FAMILY.

Jacob Forney, Sr., (sketch of his life previously given) married Mariah Bergner, a native of Switzerland. Their descendants were three sons, Jacob, Peter and Abram, and four daughters. Catherine married Abram Earhardt, Elizabeth married John Young, Christina married David Abernathy and Susan married John D. Abernathy. Of the descendants of the daughters, who left the State soon after marriage, little is known.

Jacob Forney, the eldest son, married Mary Corpening, of Burke county, N.C. Soon after the Revolutionary war he purchased a valuable track of land on Upper creek, five miles northwest of Morganton, on which he settled and raised a large family. He lived a long, quiet and useful life. His tombstone, in a private cemetery on the old homestead property, bears this inscription: "Sacred to the memory of Jacob Forney, born Nov. 6th, 1754, died Nov. 7th, 1840, aged eighty-six years and one day." He had eleven children:

1. Elizabeth E. Forney, (died young.)

2. Thomas J. Forney married S.C. Harris, of Montgomery County.

3. Isaac Newton Forney, married M.L. Corpening, of Burke County.

4. Marcus L. Forney married S. Connelly, of Burke County.

5. Albert G. Forney married Eglantine Logan, of Rutherford County.

6 Fatima E. Forney married H. Alexander Tate, of Burke County.

7. Peter Bergner Forney married M.S. Connelly, of Caldwell County.

8. James Harvey Forney married Emily Logan, of Rutherford County.

9. Daniel J. Forney married S.C. Ramsour, of Lincoln County.

10. Mary L. Forney married W.P. Reinhardt, of Catawba County.

11. Catharine S. Forney married A.T. Bost, of Catawba County.

12. *General Peter Forney*, (sketch of his life previously given) married Nancy, daughter of David Abernathy, of Lincoln County. He had twelve children:

1. Daniel M. Forney married Harriet Brevard, of Lincoln County.

2. Mary Forney married Christian Reinhardt, of Lincoln County.

3. Moses Forney, (died in Alabama unmarried.)

4. Jacob Forney married Sarah Hoke, of Lincoln County,

5. Joseph Forney (died comparatively young.)

6. Eliza Forney married 1st, Henry T. Webb, Esq., of North Carolina, and 2nd, Dr. John Meek, of Alabama.

7. Susan Forney married Bartlett Shipp, Esq., of Lincoln County.

8. Lavinia Forney married John Fulenwider, of Lincoln County.

9. Nancy Forney married Dr. William Johnston, of Lincoln County.

10. Caroline Forney married Ransom G. Hunley, of South Carolina.

11. Sophia G. Forney married Dr. C.L. Hunter, of Lincoln County.

12. J. Monroe Forney married Sarah Fulenwider, of Cleaveland County.

13. *Major Abram Forney*, (sketch of his life previously given,) married Rachel Gabriel, of Lincoln county. He only had two children:

1. Abram Earhardt Forney, a worthy citizen of the same county, and now (1876) considerably past his "three score years and ten," and 2., John W. Forney, who died comparatively young.

Daniel M. Forney, eldest son of Gen. Peter Forney, received the appointment of Major in the war of 1812, and proceeded to the scene of conflict in Canada. He served as a Representative to Congress from 1815 to 1818, and as a Senator from Lincoln county to the State Legislature from 1823 to 1826. In 1834, he moved to Lowndes County, Ala., where he died in October, 1847, in the sixty-fourth year of his age. He had seven children:

1. Eloise Forney married Gen. Jones Withers, of Mobile, Ala.

2. Mariah Forney married Judge Moore, of Alabama,

3. Alexander B. Forney, (died comparatively young.)

4. Harriet Forney, (died young.)

5. Macon Forney, (died young.)

6. Susan Forney, married Dr. B.C. Jones, of Alabama.

7. Emma Forney married Col. M. Smith, of Alabama.

2. *Mary Forney*, who married Christian Reinhardt, had five sons and four daughters. One of the sons, Franklin M. Reinhardt, who remained in the State, was a worthy member of society, highly esteemed by all who knew him, and remarkable for his benevolent disposition and liberality to the poor. He married Sarah, daughter of the late David Smith, of Lincoln County. He died on the 12th of June, 1869, in the sixty-second year of his age.

3. *Jacob Forney*, who married Sarah Hoke, daughter of the late Daniel Hoke, formerly of Lincoln County, N.C., was an enterprising, useful and highly respected member of society, possessed many noble traits of character, and raised a large and interesting family. He moved in 1835, from Lincoln County to Alabama, and settled in Jacksonville, where he died on the 24th of April, 1856, in the sixty-ninth, year of his age. He had nine children:

1. Daniel P. Forney, of Jacksonville, Alabama.

2. Joseph B. Forney married Mary Whitaker, of Alabama.

3. William H. Forney married Eliza Woodward, of Alabama.

4. Barbara Ann Forney married P. Rowan, Esq., of Alabama.

5. Gen. John H. Forney married Septima Rutledge, grand-daughter of Edward Rutledge, one of the signers of the Declaration of Independence.

6. Emma E. Forney married 1st, Col. Rice, 2nd, Rev. Thomas A. Morris.

7. Col. George H. Forney, (killed at Spotsylvania Court House, Va.)

8. Catharine Amelia Forney, married J.M. Wylie, Esq., of Alabama.

9. Mariah Louisa Forney, ("Ida") married R.D. Williams, Esq., of Alabama.

The sons of Jacob Forney won military distinction and renown in the late Confederate war. Our prescribed limits forbid a more extended notice of their gallant services. Their chivalric courage and "deeds of noble daring" will justly claim the careful study of some future historian.

4. *Eliza Forney* married 1st, Henry Y. Webb, Esq., of Granville County, N.C. He was educated at the University of North Carolina, was a member of the Legislature in 1817; appointed by President Monroe, Territorial Judge of Alabama; elected to the same position by the State Convention of 1819, and died in September, 1823.

Eliza Forney, by first marriage with Henry Y. Webb, Esq., had five children.

1. Frances Ann Webb married Col. John R. Hampton formerly of Charlotte, N.C., now a worthy and highly respected citizen of Bradley County, Ark. His wife Frances, died in 1842, leaving three children, of whom only one, (Susan) widow of Dr. Greene Newton, at present survives.

2. William P. Webb, Esq., married Martha Bell, of Alabama. His children are:

1. James E. Webb, of Hale County, Alabama, married Zemma Creswell.

2. Frances E. Webb married Robert Crawford, of St. Louis, Mo.

3. Judge William H. Webb married "Donna Louise Abrigo," of Monterey, Mexico.

4. Rev. Frank Bell Webb, pastor of the Presbyterian Church, at Union Springs, Ala.

5. Wert Webb, commission merchant of St. Louis, Mo., and two daughters, now in their minority.

3. Col. James D. Webb, of the 51st Alabama Regiment, married Jessie Walton. He was frequently a member of the Legislature of Alabama, and was highly esteemed for his purity of character. He died of wounds received in battle, July 3rd, 1863, near Winchester, Tenn., where he is buried. He left a widow and six children.

4. Susan E. Webb died in 1832, at the age of twelve years.

5. Dr. Henry Y. Webb, married Elizabeth S. Alexander, a great-grand daughter of Abraham Alexander, Chairman of the

Mecklenburg Convention of the 20th of May, 1775. Most of the Alexanders in the United States have descended from seven brothers who fled from Scotland to the North of Ireland on account of civil and religious persecutions. From 1725 to 1740, many of their descendants emigrated to America, one of whom was William Alexander, who inherited an estate and earldom in Scotland, and became Lord Stirling, a distinguished General in the Revolutionary war. After a short sojourn in Pennsylvania, many of the Alexander families and their descendants emigrated south, and formed numerous settlements in Mecklenburg and adjoining counties.

Descendants of Eliza Forney (2nd marriage) and Dr. John Meek were:

1. Samuel T. Meek, married Miss Cabeen, of South Carolina.

2. John A. Meek, of Franklin, Ky., married Miss Newton, of Arkansas.

3. Lavinia Meek married, 1st, Col. Harry Williams, of Louisiana and 2nd, E.B. Cryer, of Trenton, Louisiana.

4. Nancy, and 5, Sarah Meek.

Bartlett Shipp, who married Susan Forney, served in the State Legislature from 1824 to 1830, and was one of the delegates from Lincoln County in 1835, to amend the constitution. He was an able lawyer, had a large practice for many years, and died in Lincolnton, on the 26th of May, 1869, in the eighty fourth year of his age. His descendants were:

1. Eliza Shipp married William Preston Bynum, Esq., at present one of the Judges of the Supreme Court of North Carolina.

2. William M. Shipp, Esq., married 1st, Catharine Cameron, of Hillsboro, and 2d, Margaret Iredell, of Raleigh.

3. Susan Shipp married V.Q. Johnson, Esq., of Virginia.

Descendants of John Fulenwider and Lavinia Forney were:

1. John M. Fulenwider married Frances Hudson, of Alabama.

2. Eliza Fulenwider married L.M. Rudisill, Esq., of Catawba county, N.C.

3. Robert Fulenwider married Mary Sellers of Alabama.

4. Daniel Fulenwider married Mary Ann Leslie of Alabama.

5. Jane Fulenwider married Joshua Kirby, of Alabama.

6. Fannie Fulenwider, married James Gore, of Alabama.

7. Louisa Fulenwider married Robert Loyd, of Alabama.

8. Mary Fulenwider, (unmarried.)

For descendants of Dr. William Johnston and Nancy Forney see
"Genealogy of Colonel James Johnston."

Descendants of Ransom G. Hunley and Carolina Forney, were:

1. Richard R. Hunley married Martha S. Johnston, of Lincoln county.

2. Col. Peter F. Hunley married Margaret Johnston, of Lincoln county.

3. Mary Hunley married Gen. E.W. Martin, of Alabama.

4. Annie Hunley married Alfred Agee, Esq., of Alabama.

5. Ransom Hunley, (died young.)

Descendants of Dr. C.L. Hunter and Sophia G. Forney, were:

1. Nancy Jane Hunter, (died young.)

2. Caroline Elmina Hunter, (died young.)

3. Henry Stanhope Hunter (severely wounded in the late war.)

4. Capt. George William Hunter, mortally wounded in the battle at Chancellorsville, Va.

5. Sophia F. Hunter married John H. Sharp, Esq., of Norfolk, Va.

CHAPTER VI.

GASTON COUNTY.

Gaston County was formed in 1846, from Lincoln county, and derives its name from William Gaston, one of the most distinguished men of North Carolina, and late one of the Judges of the Supreme Court. In the language of one who knew him well (the late Chief Justice Ruffin) "he was a great Judge, and a good man." Its capital, Dallas, is named in honor of the Hon. George M. Dallas, Vice-President of the United States in 1844.

The territory embraced in this county, contained many true and gallant Whigs during the Revolutionary war. Sketches of some of these will appear in the present chapter.

REV. HUMPHREY HUNTER.

[Condensed from Wheeler's "Historical Sketches."]

Rev. Humphrey Hunter was born in Ireland, near Londonderry, on the 14th of May, 1775. His paternal grandfather was from Glasgow, in Scotland. His maternal grandfather was from Brest, in France. His descent is thus traced to the Scotch-Irish, and Huguenots of France, forming a race of people who greatly contributed to the spread of civil and religious liberty wherever their lots were cast. In America, the asylum of the oppressed of all nations, many of their descendants occupy proud positions on the page of history, and acted a magnanimous part in the achievement of our independence.

At the early age of four years, Humphrey Hunter was deprived by death of his father. In a short time afterward, his mother joined the great tide of emigration to the new world, and in May 1759, embarked on the ship Helena, bound for Charleston, S.C. After a long and boisterous voyage, the vessel at length reached its destination in safety. His mother then procured a cheap conveyance and proceeded to the eastern part of Mecklenburg County, (now in Cabarrus) where she purchased a small tract of land, and spent the remainder of her days.

In the manuscript journal of the Rev. Humphrey Hunter, we are furnished with some interesting facts respecting his life and services. He informs us he grew up in the neighborhood of Poplar Tent, inhaling the salubrious air of a free clime, and imbibing the principles of genuine liberty. At this stage of his early training, he pays a beautiful tribute to the patriotism of the mothers of the Revolution. He says:

"Neither were our mother's silent at the commencement of the Revolution." "Go son, said his mother, and join yourself to the men of our country. We ventured our lives on the waves of the ocean in quest of the freedom promised us here. Go, and fight for it, and rather let me hear of your *death* than of your *cowardice*."

In a short time afterward this patriotic advice of his mother was called into action. "Orders were presently issued," continues his journal, "by Colonel Thomas Polk to the several militia companies of the county for two men, selected from each *beat* or district to meet at the Court House in Charlotte, on the 19th day of May, 1775, in order to consult upon such measures as might be thought best to be pursued. Accordingly, on said day, a far greater number than two out of each company were present." Drawn by the great excitement of the occasion, surpassing that of any other preceding it, he attended the Convention on the appointed day. He was then a few days over twenty years of his age, and mingled with the numerous crowd of interested spectators. He then had the pleasure of listening to the reading of the *first Declaration of Independence* in the United States, and joined in the shout of approval which burst forth from the assembled multitude.

In a short time after the Convention in Charlotte, Col. Thomas Polk raised a regiment of infantry and cavalry, and marched in the direction of Cross creek (now Fayetteville) to disperse a body of Tories. In this service, he joined a corps of cavalry under Captain Chas. Polk. Soon after the return of this expedition, he commenced his classical studies at Clio Academy, in the western part of Rowan County, (now Iredell) under the instruction of the Rev. James Hall.

About this time the Cherokee Indians were committing numerous depredations and occasional murders near the head sources of the Catawba River. Upon this information, Gen. Rutherford called out a brigade of militia from Guilford, Mecklenburg, Rowan, Lincoln and other western counties, composed of infantry and three corps of cavalry.

In one of the companies commanded by Captain, afterwards Col. Robert Mebane, he acted as Lieutenant. Two skirmishes took place during this campaign, in which several Indians were killed and a considerable number made prisoners, among the latter, Hicks and Scott, two white traders, who had married Indians and espoused their cause. After his return from the Cherokee expedition, he resumed his classical education at Queen's Museum, in Charlotte, under the control of Dr. Alexander McWhorter, an eminent Presbyterian clergyman from New Jersey. In the summer of 1780, this institution, having assumed in 1777, the more patriotic name of "Liberty Hall Academy," was broken up by the approach of the British army under Lord Cornwallis. The school, then in a flourishing state, was dismissed; the young men were urged by Dr. McWhorter with patriotic appeals, to take up arms in defence of their country; and upon all he invoked the blessings of Heaven. At this time Gen. Gates was on his way to the Southern States. Under orders from Gen. Rutherford, a brigade was promptly raised to rendezvous at Salisbury. In this brigade Hunter acted for a short time as Commissary, and afterward as Lieutenant in the company of Capt. Givens.

This force first marched from Salisbury down the northeast side of the Yadkin, scouring the Tory settlements of the Uwharrie and Deep rivers, previous to its junction with Gen. Gates at Cheraw. From this place Gen. Gates moved forward to Clermont, where he arrived on the 12th of August. On the 15th he marched towards Camden, progressing as far as the Gum

Swamp, where sharp skirmishing took place in the night between advanced parties of the Americans and the British. On the 16th of August, 1780, the unfortunate battle of Camden was fought. A contagious panic seized most of the militia early in the action, and a precipitate retreat was the natural consequence.

The regulars of Maryland and Delaware, with a small portion of the North Carolina militia, firmly stood their ground until surrounded with overwhelming numbers. The subject of this sketch was there made a prisoner and stripped of most of his clothes. Soon after his surrender he witnessed the painful incidents of battle, resulting in the death of Baron DeKalb. He informs us he saw the Baron without suite or aid, and without manifesting the designs of his movements, galloping down the line. He was soon descried by the enemy, who, clapping their hands on their shoulders in reference to his epaulettes, exclaimed "a General, a rebel General." Immediately a man on horseback (not Tarleton) met him and demanded his sword. The Baron reluctantly presented the handle towards him, inquiring in French, "Are you an officer, sir." His antagonist not understanding the language, with an oath, more sternly demanded his sword. The Baron then rode on with all possible speed, disdaining to surrender to any one but an officer. Soon the cry, "a rebel General," sounded along the line.

The musketeers immediately, by platoons, fired upon him. He proceeded about twenty-five rods, when he fell from his horse, mortally wounded. Presently he was raised to his feet, stripped of his hat, coat and neck-cloth, and placed with his hands resting on a wagon. His body was found, upon examination, to have been pierced by seven musket balls. Whilst standing in this position, and the blood streaming through his shirt, Cornwallis, with his suite, rode up.

106

Being informed that the wounded man was Baron De Kalb, he addressed him by saying: "I am sorry, sir, to see you; not sorry that you are vanquished, but sorry to see you so badly wounded." Having given orders to an officer to administer to the wants of the Baron, Cornwallis rode on to secure the fruits of his victory. In a short time the brave and generous De Kalb, who had served in the armies of France and embarked in the American cause, breathed his last. He is buried in Camden, where a neat monument has been erected to his memory.

After being confined seven days in a prison-yard in Camden, Hunter was taken, with many other prisoners, including about fifty officers, to Orangeburg, where he remained until the 13th of November following, *without hat or coat*. On that day, without any intention of transgressing, he set out to visit a friendly lady in the suburbs who had promised to give him a homespun coat. Before he reached her residence, he was stopped by a horseman, armed with sword and pistols, who styled himself a Lieutenant of the station at the Court House, under Col. Fisher. The horseman blustered and threatened, and sternly commanded him to march before him to the station to be tried for having broken his parole. No excuse, apology or confession would be received in extenuation of his transgression. "To the station," said the horseman, "you shall go—take the road." The Tory loyalist was evidently exercising his brief authority over a real Whig.

Up the road his prisoner had to go, sour and sulky, with much reluctance, being hurried in his march by the point of the Tory's sword. Hunter pursued his course, but constantly on the look-out for some means of self-defence. Fortunately, after they progressed a short distance, they approached a large fallen pine tree, around which lay a quantity of pine-knots, hardened and blackened by the recent action of fire. Hunter, in an instant, saw "his opportunity," immediately jumped to the further side of said tree, and, armed with a good pine-knot, prepared for combat. The Tory instantly fired one of his pistols at him, but without effect. He then leaped his horse over the tree.

Hunter, with equal promptness, exchanged sides, being fired at a second time by his would-be conqueror, but again without effect. Much skilful maneuvering took place, whilst the Tory was thus kept at bay. Hunter then commenced a vigorous warfare with the pine-knots so opportunely placed at his command, and dealt them out with profuse liberality. The accurate aim of two or three pine-knots against the horseman's head soon disabled him and brought him to the ground. He was then disarmed of his sword, and capitulated on the following terms: That Hunter should never make known the conquest he had gained over him, and give back the captured sword; and that he, (the Tory loyalist) would never report to headquarters that any of the prisoners had ever crossed the boundary line, or offended in any other manner. But secrecy could not be preserved, for during the combat the horse, without his rider, galloped off to the station and created considerable anxiety respecting the horseman's fate.

All serious apprehensions, however, were soon removed as the dismounted horseman presently made his appearance, with several visible bruises on his head, bearing striking proof of the effective precision of the pine-knots. A close examination was soon instituted at the station, and numerous searching questions propounded to the wounded horseman, when the history of the contest had to be given, and all concealment no longer attempted.

The encounter took place on a Friday evening. On the Sabbath following, orders were issued by Col. Fisher to all the prisoners to appear at the Court House on Monday by twelve o'clock. On the evening of that Sabbath, Hunter, expecting close confinement, or, perhaps, the loss of his life, made his escape with five or six others from Mecklenburg, and commenced their way to North Carolina.

They concealed themselves by day to avoid the British scouts sent in pursuit, and traveled during the night, supporting themselves principally on the *raw corn* found by the way-side. On the ninth night after they set out from Orangeburg, they crossed the Catawba and arrived safely in Mecklenburg county.

After remaining a few days at his mother's residence, he again entered the service, and joined a cavalry company, acting as lieutenant under Colonel Henry Lee. In a short time, the battle of the Eutaw Springs, the last important one in the extreme South, took place. In this engagement, where so much personal bravery was displayed, he performed a gallant part, and was slightly wounded. With this campaign, his military services ended. Among the variety of incidents which occurred during this year he was gratified in revisiting his old prison-bounds, and in witnessing the reduction of the station at Orangeburg. But greater still was the gratification he experienced in again beholding the identical sword he had taken from his Tory antagonist, as previously stated.

Soon after the close of the war he resumed his classical studies under the instruction of the Rev. Robert Archibald, near Poplar Tent Church. During the summer of 1785, he entered the Junior Class at Mount Zion College, in Winnsboro, S.C., and graduated in July, 1787. In a short time afterward he commenced the study of Theology under the care of the Presbytery of South Carolina, and was licensed to preach in October, 1789.

In 1796 he removed from South Carolina to the south-eastern part of Lincoln county (now Gaston) where he purchased a home for his rising family. His ministerial labors extended through a period of nearly thirty-eight years, principally at Goshen and Unity churches in Lincoln county (under its old boundaries) and Steele Creek church, in Mecklenburg county. In 1789 he married Jane, daughter of Dr. George Ross, of Laurens District, S.C.—an estimable lady, noted for her amiable disposition, numerous acts of charity, and fervent piety.

In his preaching Mr. Hunter was earnest, persuasive and often eloquent. He possessed, in a remarkable degree, a talent for refined sarcasm, and knew how to use most effectively its piercing shafts against the idle objections, or disingenuous cavils of all triflers with the great truths of religion. In his advanced years the infirmities of old age greatly contracted the extent of his useful labors without impairing the vigor of his mental powers or the fervency and faithfulness of his preaching. He died, with Christian resignation, on the 21st of August, 1827, in the 73rd year of his age. The Rev. Humphrey Hunter had ten children, of whom, at the present time (1876) only one, the author and compiler of these sketches, survives.

DR. WILLIAM McLEAN.

Dr. William McLean was born in Rowan County, N.C., on the 2nd day of April, 1757. His father, Alexander McLean, was a native of Ireland, who emigrated to America, landing at Philadelphia, between the years 1725 and 1730. Some time after his arrival in Pennsylvania he married Elizabeth Ratchford, whose father emigrated from England shortly after McLean left Ireland. Three of his daughters, Jane, Margaret and Agnes, were born in that State. He then joined the great tide of emigration to the more enticing fields and genial climate of the southern colonies, and settled in the Dobbin neighborhood, eight miles from Salisbury, Rowan County, N.C.

Here he remained for a few years, during which time his eldest son John, and William, the immediate subject of this sketch, were born. He then moved to a tract of land he purchased near the junction of the South Fork with the main Catawba river, in Tryon, (now Gaston county,) where three more sons were born, Alexander, George and Thomas. This place he made his permanent abode during the remainder of his life, surrounded with the greater portion of his rising family. He attained a good old age, his wife surviving him a few years; both were consistent members of the Presbyterian Church, and are buried at the old "Smith graveyard," near the place of his last settlement.

Soon after the Revolutionary war, Alexander McLean, Jr., moved to Missouri, and George McLean to Tennessee. Thomas McLean, the youngest son, retained the old homestead, where, at an advanced age, he ended his earthly existence. Although only thirteen years old at the time of the battle of King's Mountain, he could give a glowing account of the heroic bravery which characterized that brilliant victory in which many of his neighbors, under the brave Lieut. Col. Hambright and Maj. Chronicle, actively participated. John McLean, the eldest son, performed a soldier's duty on several occasions during the war.

Upon the call of troops from North Carolina for the defence of Charleston, he attached himself to Col. Graham's regiment, under Gen. Rutherford, and was there captured. Immediately after being exchanged, he returned to North Carolina and joined the command of Capt. Adlai Osborne, and about three month's afterward was killed in a skirmish at Buford's Bridge, S.C.

After the removal of Alexander McLean to his final settlement on the south fork of the Catawba, as previously stated, William assisted him on the farm, and when a favorable opportunity offered, went to school in the neighborhood, acquiring as good an education as the facilities of the country then afforded. His instructor for the last three months in this early training was a Mr. Blythe, who, noticing his rapid advancement in learning, and capacity for more extended usefulness, advised him to go to Queen's Museum, in Charlotte. This institution was then in high repute under the able management of Dr. Alexander and Rev. Alexander McWhorter, a distinguished Presbyterian clergyman from New Jersey.

Dr. McLean complied with the advice of his instructor, and became a pupil of Queen's Museum. In this venerated institution, shedding abroad its enlightening influence on Western North Carolina, many of the leading patriots of the Revolution acquired their principal educational training.

Its president, Dr. McWhorter, was not only an eminent preacher of the gospel, but was also an ardent patriot, and never failed, on suitable occasions, to discuss the politics of the day, and instil into the minds of his youthful pupils the essential principles of civil and religious liberty. His sentiments in this respect were so generally known, that it is said Cornwallis previous to his entrance into Charlotte in 1780, was extremely anxious to *enfold him in his embraces.*

Dr. McLean remained in this institution of learning about two years and then returned home. Having made up his mind to become a physician during his collegiate course, he gathered all the medical books he could procure at that period, and diligently devoted his time to their study. In this stage of his early preparation for future usefulness, Dr. Joseph Blythe, a distinguished surgeon in the Continental Army, wrote to him in terms of warmest friendship, and offered him the position of "surgeon's mate."

This offer he accepted, repaired to Charlotte, and they both marched with the army to James Island, near Charleston. In this immediate vicinity at Stono (the narrow river or inlet, which separates John's Island from the main land) a severe but indecisive battle had been fought between a detachment of General Lincoln's army and the British, under General Prevost, in June, 1779.

At the time of Dr. McLean's arrival at James Island, many soldiers were sick with the pestilential "camp fever" of that sultry climate, or were suffering from the wounds of battle at the army hospital. Some of these sufferers were from Lincoln and Mecklenburg counties, with whom he was personally acquainted. Under judicious medical treatment he was pleased to see most of them, in a short time, restored to health and ready for the future service of their country.

In the summer and fall of 1780 Dr. McLean was constantly with the Southern army watching the movements of Ferguson in the upper Tory settlements of South Carolina, previous to his defeat and death at King's Mountain. After that battle he went to Charlotte to wait on the sick and the wounded at that place.

In 1781 he was with General Greene's army, near Camden, and at other military encampments requiring his services. In all of these responsible positions he continued to faithfully discharge the duties of "Surgeon's Mate," or Assistant Surgeon, until the close of the Revolution.

Having completed his preparatory studies Dr. McLean went to the medical University of Pennsylvania at Philadelphia, and received from that venerable institution his diploma in 1787. In a short time after his arrival at home he purchased a farm in the "South Point" neighborhood, soon engaged in an extensive practice (frequently charitable) and became eminent in his profession.

On the 19th of June, 1792, Dr. McLean married Mary, daughter of Major John Davidson, one of the signers of the Mecklenburg Declaration of Independence. In 1814 he was elected to the Senate from Lincoln County. In 1815 he delivered an address at King's Mountain, commemorative of the battle at that place, and caused to be erected, at his own expense, a plain headstone of dark slate rock, with appropriate inscriptions on both sides. The inscription on the east side reads thus: "Sacred to the memory of Major William Chronicle, Capt. John Mattocks, William Robb and John Boyd, who were killed here on the 7th of October, 1780, fighting in defence of America."

The inscription on the west side reads thus: "Colonel Ferguson, an officer belonging to his Brittanic Majesty, was here defeated and killed."

Dr. McLean, after a life of protracted usefulness, died with peaceful resignation on the 25th of October, 1828, in the seventy-second year of his age. His wife survived him many years, being nearly ninety-seven years old at the time of her death. They were both long, worthy and consistant members of the Presbyterian church, dignified their lives with their professions, and are buried in Bethel Graveyard, York County, S.C.

MAJOR WILLIAM CHRONICLE.

Major William Cronicle, the soldier and martyr to the cause of liberty at King's Mountain, was born in the south eastern part of Lincoln county (now Gaston) about 1755. His mother was first married to a Mr. McKee in Pennsylvania, who afterwards removed to North Carolina and settled in Mecklenburg county. By this marriage she had one son, James McKee, a soldier of the revolution, and ancestor of the several families of that name in the neighborhood of Armstrong's Ford, on the South Fork of the Catawba.

After McKee's death, his widow married Mr. Chronicle, by whom she had an only son, William, who afterward performed a magnanimous part in defence of his country's rights. The site of the old family mansion is still pointed out by the oldest inhabitants with feelings of lingering veneration. "There," they will tell you, "is the spot where old Mr. Chronicle lived and his brave son, William, was brought up." The universal testimony of all who knew Major Chronicle represented him as the constant, never-tiring advocate of liberty, and as exerting a powerful influence in spreading the principles of freedom throughout the whole lower portion of old Lincoln county. His jovial turn of mind and winning manners, by gaining the good will of all, greatly assisted in making successful his appeals to their patriotism, and promoting the cause of liberty in which he had so zealously embarked.

Major Chronicle's first service was performed as Captain of a company at Purysburg in South Carolina. Early in the fall of 1780, a regiment was raised in Lincoln County, over which Col. William Graham was appointed Colonel; Frederick Hambrite, Lieut. Colonel, and William Chronicle, Major. It is well known that Col. Graham, on account of severe sickness in his family, was not present at the battle of King's Mountain.

117

The immediate command of the regiment, assisted by Col. Dickson of the county, was then gallantly assumed by these officers, and nobly did they sustain themselves by word and example, in that ever-memorable conflict.

Major Chronicle was brave, perhaps to a fault, energetic in his movements, self possessed in danger, and deeply imbued with the spirit of liberty. His last words of encouragement in leading a spirited charge against the enemy, were "Come on my boys, never let it be said a Fork boy run," alluding to South Fork, near which stream most of them resided.

This patriotic appeal was not given in vain. It nerved every man for the contest. Onward his brave boys steadily moved forward, Major Chronicle in the advance, and approached within gun-shot of the British forces. Just at this time, a few sharp shooters of the enemy discharged their pieces, and retreated. The brave Chronicle fell mortally wounded, receiving a fatal ball in the breast. Almost at the same time, Capt. John Mattocks and Lieutenants William Rabb and John Boyd, also fell. Major Chronicle was only about twenty-five years old at the time of his death. The late Capt. Samuel Caldwell and his brother William, were both in this battle. William Caldwell brought home Major Chronicle's horse; his sword and spurs passed into the hands of his half brother, James McKee, and the venerated memorials are still in possession of one of his sons, who moved many years ago to Tennessee.

CAPTAIN SAMUEL MARTIN.

Captain Samuel Martin was a native of Ireland, and born in the year 1732. When a young man, he emigrated to America, and first settled in Pennsylvania. After remaining a short time in that State, he joined the great tide of emigration to the southern colonies. He first entered the service as a private in Captain Robert Alexander's company, in June 1776, Colonel Graham's Regiment, and marched to Fort McGaughey, in Rutherford County, and thence across the Blue Ridge Mountains against the Cherokee Indians, who were committing murders and depredations upon the frontier settlements. In January 1777, he attached himself to the command of Captain William Chronicle, and marched to the relief of the post of Ninety Six, in Abbeville County, S.C., and after this service he returned to North Carolina.

About the 1st of November, 1779, his company was ordered to Charlotte, at that time a place of rendezvous of soldiers for the surrounding counties, and while there he received a special commission of captain, conferred on him by General Rutherford. With his special command he marched with other forces from Charlotte by way of Camden, to the relief of Charleston, and fell in with Col. Hampton, at the Governor's gate, near that city. Finding that place completely invested by the British army, he remained but a short time, and returned to North Carolina with Colonel Graham's regiment, about the 1st of June, 1780.

Being informed on the night of his arrival at home that the Tories were embodied in strong force at Ramsour's Mill, near the present town of Lincolnton, he immediately raised a small company and joined General Davidson's battalion, General Rutherford commanding, encamped at Colonel Dickson's plantation, three miles northwest of Tuckaseege ford. General

119

Rutherford broke up his encampment at that place, early on the morning of the 20th of June, 1780, then sixteen miles from Ramsour's Mill, and marched with his forces, expecting to unite with Colonel Locke in making a joint attack upon the Tories, but failed to reach the scene of conflict until two hours after the battle. The Tories had been signally defeated and routed by Colonel Locke and his brave associates, and about fifty made prisoners, among the number a brother of Colonel Moore, the commander of the Tory forces.

Immediately after this battle he received orders from Colonels Johnston and Dickson to proceed with his company to Colonel Moore's residence, six or seven miles west of the present town of Lincolnton, and arrest that Tory leader, but he had fled with about thirty of his follower's to Camden, S.C., where Cornwallis was then encamped. Soon after this service Captain Martin was ordered to proceed with his company to Rugeley's Mill, in Kershaw County, S.C. Here Colonel Rugeley, the Tory commander, had assembled a considerable force, and fortified his log barn and dwelling house. Colonel Washington, by order of General Morgan, had pursued him with his cavalry, but having no artillery, he resorted to an ingenious stratagem to capture the post without sacrificing his own men.

Accordingly he mounted a *pine log*, fashioned as a cannon, elevated on its own limbs, and placed it in position to command the houses in which the Tories were lodged. Colonel Washington then made a formal demand for immediate surrender. Colonel Rugeley fearing the destructive consequences of the formidable cannon bearing upon his command in the log barn and dwelling house, after a stipulation as to terms, promptly surrendered his whole force, consisting of one hundred and twelve men, without a gun being fired on either side. It was upon the reception of the news of this surrender that Cornwallis wrote to Tarleton, "Rugeley will not be made a Brigadier."

After this successful stratagem, seldom equaled during the war, Captain Martin was ordered to march with his company in pursuit of Colonel Cunningham, (commonly called "bloody Bill Cunningham") a Tory leader, encamped on Fishing creek, but he fled so rapidly he could not overtake him.

During the latter part of August and the whole of September, Captain Martin was rarely at home, and then not remaining for more than two days at a time. About the last week of September he marched with his company by a circuitous route, under Colonel Graham, to the Cowpens. There he united with Colonels Campbell, Shelby, Sevier, Cleaveland and other officers and marched with them to King's Mountain. In this battle Captain Martin acted a conspicuous part, was in the *thickest of the fight*, and lost six of his company. After this battle he continued in active scouting duties wherever his services were needed.

When Cornwallis marched through Lincoln County in pursuit of General Morgan, encumbered with upwards of five hundred prisoners, captured at the Cowpens, he was ordered to harass his advance as much as possible. A short time after Cornwallis crossed the Catawba at Cowan's Ford, he marched as far as Salisbury, when he was ordered by Colonel Dickson to convey some prisoners to Charlotte. Having performed this service, he proceeded to Guilford Court house, but did not reach that place until after the battle. He then returned home, and was soon after discharged.

In October 1833, Captain Martin, when *one hundred and one years* old, was granted a pension by the general government. He was a worthy and consistent member of the Associate

Reformed Church, and died on the 26th of November, 1836, aged *one hundred and four years!* He married in Ireland, Margaret McCurdy, who also attained an extreme old age, and both are buried in Goshen graveyard, in Gaston county.

CAPTAIN SAMUEL CALDWELL.

Samuel Caldwell was born in Orange County, N.C., on the 10th of February, 1759, and moved to Tryon County, afterward Lincoln, in 1772. He first entered the service in Captain Gowen's company in 1776, and marched against the Cherokee Indians beyond the mountains. In 1779, he volunteered (in Captain William Chronicle's company) in the "nine months service," and joined General Lincoln's army at Purysburg, S.C. In March, 1780, he joined Captain Isaac White's company, and marched to King's Mountain. In the battle which immediately followed, he and his brother, William actively participated.

Shortly after this celebrated victory, he attached himself to Captain Montgomery's company and was in the battle of the Cowpens, fought on the 17th of January, 1781. Soon afterward he marched to Guilford, and was in the battle fought there on the 15th of March, 1781. In the following fall, he substituted for Clement Nance, in Captain Lemmonds cavalry company in the regiment commanded by Col. Robert Smith and Major Joseph Graham.

At the Raft Swamp, they attacked and signally defeated a large body of Tories; and in two days afterward defeated a band of Tories on Alfred Moore's plantation opposite Wilmington. On the next day, the same troops made a vigorous attack on the garrison, near the same place. After this service, he returned home and was frequently engaged in other minor but important military duties until the close of the war.

After the war, Captain Caldwell settled on a farm three miles southwest of Tuckaseege Ford where he raised a large family. He was a kind and obliging neighbor, attained a good old age, and is buried in the graveyard of Goshen church, Gaston county N.C.

CAPTAIN JOHN MATTOCKS.

Captain John Mattocks was one of the brave soldiers who fell at King's Mountain. He belonged to a family who resided a few miles below Armstrong's Ford, on the south fork of the Catawba river, at what is now known as the "Alison old place." There were three brothers and two sisters, Sallie and Barbara. The whole family, men and women, had the reputation of being "*uncommonly stout.*" John and Charles Mattocks were staunch Whigs, ever ready to engage in any enterprise in defence of the freedom of their country, but Edward Mattocks (commonly called Ned Mattocks) was a Tory.

All of the brothers were at the battle of King's Mountain, in which Captain Charles Mattocks was killed early in the action when pressing forward with undaunted courage against the enemy. Among the severely wounded, was Ned Mattocks, the Tory brother. After the battle and signal victory, Charles Mattocks, fearing his brother might be hung with some others who suffered this penalty on the next day, kindly interceded in his behalf, took him home and nursed him carefully until he recovered of his wound.

It is said, this *extraction of blood* so effectually performed by some one of the gallant Whigs on that occasion, completely *cured* Ned Mattocks of *Toryism* and caused him never afterward to unite with the enemies of his country. The whole surviving family a few years after the war moved to Georgia, where they have descendants at the present time.

Major Chronicle, Captain Mattocks, William Rabb and John Boyd, all from the same South Fork neighborhood, are buried in a common grave at the foot of the mountain.

A plain head-stone of dark slate rock, commemorates the hallowed spot with the following inscription:

"Sacred to the memory of
MAJOR WILLIAM CHRONICLE,
CAPTAIN JOHN MATTOCKS,
WILLIAM RABB,
JOHN BOYD,

"Who were killed here fighting in defence of America, On the
7th of October, 1780."

Many fragmentary but interesting incidents connected with the battle of King's Mountain have come down to our own time and unfortunately, many others have been buried in oblivion. The following incident was related to the author by a grandson of a brave soldier in that battle. Moses and James Henry both actively participated in that hotly contested engagement.

A few days after the battle, as James Henry was passing through the woods near the scene of conflict, he found a very fine horse, handsomely equipped with an elegant saddle, the reins of the bridle being broken. The horse and equipments were, as he supposed, the property of an officer. He took the horse home with him, considerably elated with his good luck; but his mother met him at the gate, and immediately inquired whose horse it was he had in charge, he replied, he supposed it belonged to some British officer. "James," said the mother, "turn it loose and drive it off from the place, for I will not have the hands of my household stained with British plunder."

The incident illustrates the noble Christian spirit which actuated our good mothers of the Revolutionary period.

The other brother, Moses Henry, evinced great bravery in the same engagement, and was mortally wounded. He was taken to the hospital in Charlotte, and was attentively waited upon by Dr. William McLean until he died. His widow, with several others under similar bereavement, was granted a liberal allowance by the county court of Lincoln. Moses Henry is the grandfather of Col. Moses Henry Hand, a worthy citizen of Gaston County, N.C.

WILLIAM RANKIN.

William Rankin was born in Pennsylvania, on the 10th of January, 1761, and at an early age joined the tide of emigration to the Southern States, and settled in "Tryon," afterward Lincoln County, N.C.

He first entered the service as a private in Captain Robert Alexander's company, Colonel William Graham's regiment, and marched to Montfort's Cove against the Cherokee Indians. In 1779 he volunteered under the same officer, and marched by way of Charlotte and Camden to the relief of Charleston, but finding the city completely invested by the British army, the regiment returned to North Carolina. In 1780, he again volunteered under Major Dickson, and marched against Col. Floyd, a Tory leader of upper South Carolina.

After this service he returned home, and soon afterward marched under the same officer, General Rutherford commanding, to Ramsour's Mill, where a large body of Tories had assembled under Colonel John Moore. The forces under General Rutherford were encamped on Colonel Dickson's plantation, three miles north-west of Tuckaseege Ford, and about sixteen miles from Ramsour's. Early on the morning of the 20th of June, 1780, they broke up camp and moved forward, but did not reach the battle-field until two hours after the action had taken place, and the Tories defeated by Colonel Locke and his brave associates, with a force greatly inferior to that of the enemy. Immediately after this battle, he substituted for Henry E. Locke, in Captain William Armstrong's company, marched to Park's Mill, near Charlotte, and thence to General Rutherford's army, encamped at Phifer's plantation.

The Tories having assembled a considerable force at Coulson's Mill, General Davidson with a detachment of troops vigorously attacked them, in which skirmish he (Davidson) was severely wounded, detaining him from the service about two months. Soon afterward he marched with General Rutherford's command to Camden and participated in the unfortunate battle at that place on the 16th of August, 1780. While the British army were in Charlotte he served under Captain Forney and Major Dickson, watching the movements of the enemy. Shortly afterward he volunteered under Captain James Little, marched to Rocky Mount, and thence to the Eutaw Springs. In this battle, one of the most severely contested during the Revolution, his company was placed under the command of Colonel Malmedy, a Frenchman. Soon after his return home he was placed in charge of a considerable number of prisoners, and in obedience to orders, conveyed them to Salisbury. Here he remained until his time of service expired, and then received his discharge from Colonel Locke.

William Rankin attained the good old age of nearly ninety-three, and was at the time of his death the last surviving soldier of the Revolution in Gaston County. He married Mary Moore, a sister of General John Moore, also a soldier of the Revolution. His wife preceded him several years to the tomb.

His son, Colonel Richard Rankin, is now (1876) living at the old homestead, having passed "his three score years and ten." He served several times in the State Legislature, is an industrious farmer and worthy citizen of Gaston county.

GEN. JOHN MOORE.

General John Moore was born in Lincoln county, when a part of Anson, in 1759. His father, William Moore, of Scotch-Irish descent, was one of the first settlers of the county and a prominent member of society. He had four sons, James, William, John and Alexander, who, inheriting the liberty-loving principles of that period, were all true patriots in the Revolutionary war.

John Moore performed a soldier's duty on several occasions and was one of the guards stationed at Tuckaseege Ford, watching the movements of Lord Cornwallis after his entrance into Lincoln County. He also acted for a considerable length of time as Commissary to the army. General Moore married a sister of General John Adair, of Kentucky, by whom he had many children. Several years after her death, he married Mary Scott, widow of James Scott, and daughter of Captain Robert Alexander by whom he had two children, Lee Alexander and Elizabeth Moore. He was a member of the House of Commons as early as 1788, and served for many years subsequently with great fidelity and to the general acceptance of his constituents.

To remove a false impression, sometimes entertained by persons little conversant with our Revolutionary history, it should be here stated that General John Moore was in no way related to the *Colonel John Moore*, (son of Moses Moore), who lived about seven miles west of Lincolton, and commanded the Tory forces in the battle of Ramsour's Mill.

General Moore, after a life of protracted usefulness, died in 1836, with Christian resignation, aged about seventy-seven years, and lies buried near several of his kindred in Goshen graveyard, Gaston county, N.C.

ELISHA WITHERS.

Elisha Withers was born in Stafford County, Va., on the 10th of August, 1762. His first service in the Revolutionary war was in 1780, acting for twelve months as Commissary in furnishing provisions for the soldiers stationed at Captain Robert Alexander's, near the Tuckaseege Ford on the Catawba river, their place of rendezvous. After this service, he was drafted and served a tour of three months under Captain Thomas Loftin and Lieut. Robert Shannon, and marched from Lincoln County to Guilford Court-house under Colonels Locke and Hunt. His time having expired shortly before the battle, he returned home.

He again served another tour, commencing in August, 1781, as a substitute for James Withers, under Captain James Little, at the Eutaw Springs, where he was detailed with a few others, to guard the baggage wagons during the battle. He again volunteered under Captain Thomas Loftin and Lieut. Thomas McGee and was actively engaged in the "horse service," in several scouting expeditions until the close of the war.

After the war, he was for a long time known as "old Constable Withers," was highly respected, and died at a good old age.

Appendix

The Tryon Resolves, Signed August 14, 1775

The Tryon Resolves is among the earliest documents pledging support for the North American Colonies after the Battle of Lexington, Massachusetts.

It pre-dates the Declaration of Independence by about eleven months. As tensions continue to rise, many of the signers of the Tryon Resolves formed Committees of Safety. The Tryon County Militia was formed on September 14, 1775.

Text of the Tryon Resolves

The unprecedented, barbarous and bloody actions committed by British troops on our American brethren near Boston, on 19 April and 20th of May last, together with the hostile operations and treacherous designs now carrying on, by the tools of ministerial vengeance, for the subjugation of all British America, suggest to us the painful necessity of having recourse to arms in defense of our National freedom and constitutional rights, against all invasions; and at the same time do solemnly engage to take up arms and risk our lives and our fortunes in maintaining the freedom of our country whenever the wisdom and counsel of the Continental Congress or our Provincial Convention shall declare it necessary; and this engagement we will continue in for the preservation of those rights and liberties which the principals of our Constitution and the laws of God, nature and nations have made it our duty to defend.

We therefore, the subscribers, freeholders and inhabitants of Tryon County, do here by faithfully unite ourselves under the most solemn ties of religion, honor and love to our county, firmly to resist force by force, and hold sacred till a reconciliation shall take place between Great Britain and America on Constitutional principals, which we most ardently desire, and do firmly agree to hold all such persons as inimical to the liberties of America who shall refuse to sign this association.

Signers

John Walker, Charles McLean, Andrew Neel, Thomas Beatty, James Coburn, Frederick Hambright, Andrew Hampton Benjamin Hardin, George Paris, William Graham Robt. Alexander, David Jenkins, Thomas Espey, Perrygreen Mackness (or Magness), James McAfee William Thompson, Jacob Forney, Davis Whiteside John Beeman, John Morris, Joseph Hardin, John Robison, James McIntyre, Valentine Mauney, George Black, Jas. Logan Jas. Baird, Christian Carpenter, Abel Beatty, Joab Turner Jonathan Price, Jas. Miller, John Dellinger, Peter Sides William Whiteside, Geo. Dellinger, Samuel Carpenter Jacob Mauney, Jun., John Wells, Jacob Costner, Robert Hulclip, James Buchanan, Moses Moore, Joseph Kuykendall, Adam Simms, Richard Waffer, Samuel Smith, Joseph Neel, Samuel Loftin

Other Books by Stephen Payseur

Available on Amazon.com

The Book of Daniel

A.D. The Fate of the Apostles of Christ after the Crucifixion

Narrative of the Life of David Crockett of the State of Tennessee

Lessons from the Creek

Reflections from the Creek

The North Carolina Slave Narratives Vol. 1

The North Carolina Slave Narratives Vol. 2

Made in the USA
Charleston, SC
03 June 2016